GEORGE LEONARD holds a fifth-degree black belt in aikido. He is
the president of the Esalen Institute and the founder of Leonard
Energy Training (LET), a practice inspired by aikido, which
offers alternative ways of coping with everyday problems. He has
introduced LET to more than 50,000 people in the United
States and abroad. Leonard is the author of numerous books on
human possibility and social change, including *Education and
Ecstasy*, *The Transformation*, *The Ultimate Athlete*, *The Silent
Pulse*, *Adventures in Monogamy*, and *Mastery*. He lives in northern California.

OTHER BOOKS BY GEORGE LEONARD

The Decline of the American Male (with William Attwood
and J Robert Moskin)
Shoulder the Sky (a novel)
Education and Ecstasy
The Man & Woman Thing, and Other Provocations
The Transformation
The Ultimate Athlete
The Silent Pulse
The End of Sex
Walking on the Edge of the World
Mastery
The Life We Are Given (with Michael Murphy)

The
Way of Aikido

LIFE LESSONS FROM AN AMERICAN SENSEI

George Leonard

A PLUME BOOK

PLUME
Published by the Penguin Group
Penguin Putnam Inc., 375 Hudson Street, New York, New York 10014, U.S.A.
Penguin Books Ltd, 27 Wrights Lane, London W8 5TZ, England
Penguin Books Australia Ltd, Ringwood, Victoria, Australia
Penguin Books Canada Ltd, 10 Alcorn Avenue, Toronto, Ontario, Canada M4V 3B2
Penguin Books (N.Z.) Ltd, 182–190 Wairau Road, Auckland 10, New Zealand

Penguin Books Ltd, Registered Offices: Harmondsworth, Middlesex, England

Published by Plume, a member of Penguin Putnam Inc.
Previously published in a Dutton edition.

First Plume Printing, June 2000
10 9 8 7 6

Ⓡ REGISTERED TRADEMARK—MARCA REGISTRADA

The Library of Congress has catalogued the Dutton edition as follows:
Leonard, George Burr
The way of aikido   life lessons from an American sensei / George Leonard.
    p.   cm.
    ISBN 0-525-94413-3 (hc.)
        0-452-27972-0 (pbk.)
    1. Aikido—Psychological aspects.   I. Title.
    GV1114.35.L46   1999
    796.815'4—dc21   98-54339
                                                          CIP

Printed in the United States of America
Original hardcover design by Eve L. Kirch

dressed in white jackets and black or dark blue floor-length skirts attacking their partners and being thrown to the mat. Let your ears adjust to the swish of bare feet on the lustrous blue-gray vinyl mat cover, the percussive sound of hands slapping the mat to help break falls. Let your mind accept the fact that there is some order in this seemingly random motion and that somehow, despite your immediate fears, there will be no collisions among the rushing, swarming men and women before you.

Now that your senses are adjusting, pick out a twosome, perhaps the one practicing closest to you, a muscular, balding man and a slim woman with dark hair. The man rushes at her with the real intent to bring a strong blow directly down on her head. The woman moves toward her attacker, then, at the last moment, shifts to one side so that the strike misses her by perhaps two inches. As his hand passes, she deftly brings it down even faster with one of her hands, at the same time turning her hips so as to lift his other elbow with her other hand. The man flips in midair, his momentum carrying him another six or seven feet before he crashes to the mat with an explosive slap of his hand. You find yourself starting violently. Surely, after such a fall, the man must be seriously injured. But no, he leaps to his feet and comes at his training partner again, wearing the broadest of grins on his face.

Let your gaze sweep the whole mat. Yes, almost everyone is smiling. And except for the slap of hands, the crash of bodies onto the mat, and an occasional *ki-ai* shout, the predominant sound is an occasional laugh of delight. That's what's most disorienting. All these men and women, all

CHAPTER 1

Welcome to Our Dojo

Come visit our aikido school, our dojo. Climb two flights of exterior stairs to a small outdoor landing. Open the door and walk in; visitors are always welcome. Don't be surprised if at first your senses are stunned by what you behold; a large, rectangular open space; exposed rafters on which lights are mounted; walls of soft white on which are hung framed examples of Japanese calligraphy; a sort of altar with flowers, chimes, and a large black-and-white photograph of a venerable Japanese martial artist with a white beard. But it's not the serene setting that overwhelms your senses, but rather the grand melee that is taking place within it. This is especially true if you should enter during a period of *jiyu-waza* (freestyle), where almost anything goes.

Just relax and have a seat on one of the benches for visitors. Let your eyes adjust to the swirling motion, the spectacle of some twenty or thirty men and women of various ages

The Way of Aikido

able change. I'm convinced—and I feel you will be, too—that if more people followed the clear and simple guidelines of aikido's philosophy, we would all live in a more harmonious, more beneficent world.

by its graceful movements and the stupendous variety of its techniques. But even more significant for our times than the physical art is the philosophy behind it. To understand this philosophy, to begin to live it, is to enter a world completely new, a world in which age-old assumptions are turned upside down: Contexts change, life's unanticipated blows become gifts, attacks lead to reconciliation, discord is transformed into harmony, anxiety and pain are reborn as vital energy.

Three years after taking up aikido, encouraged by my first teacher, I began including mind-body exercises in my workshop sessions, exercises inspired by aikido yet designed for nonaikidoists. Over the years, these exercises have evolved into a body of work called Leonard Energy Training (LET). I've had the opportunity to introduce this work to more than fifty thousand people, many of whom have urged me to make LET more widely available in written form. In this book I do just that, presenting the fundamentals of LET along with teaching stories that tell how I and other people have used the philosophy of aikido to better deal with stress, anxiety, and pain; to create positive outcomes out of negative situations, and to find more love, power, and joy in daily life.

I hope this book will be of service to fellow aikido students and teachers by enhancing their experience on and off the training mat. But it is primarily addressed to those who may never take up a martial art. The practical and effective philosophy I'm offering in these pages has changed my own and other people's lives for the better in many ways. It is especially useful in maintaining balance, centeredness, and composure in times of crisis, times of rapid and unpredict-

INTRODUCTION

A Revolutionary
Martial Art

Aikido, the most recent and fastest growing of the major martial arts, is also the most revolutionary. Supremely physical, it is at essence purely spiritual. Its name means literally "harmony spirit way," or poetically "the way of harmonizing with the spirit of the universe." With ancient samurai roots, it is a radical reform of the samurai tradition, seeking not victory over others but rather, in the founder's words, "the loving protection of all beings." Its techniques can cause severe damage or even death, but its heartfelt aim is peace and harmony. Truly mystical, at times seemingly paranormal, it is also eminently practical, with nearly endless applications for home, school, and office—for every aspect of our physical, emotional, social, and spiritual life.

When a friend invited me to join an aikido class he was organizing, I had never heard of the art. Now, twenty-eight years later, I am more deeply involved than ever, intoxicated

12. Blending with *Ki*   104

13. Meditation in Action   113

14. *Zanshin*. Continuing Awareness   120

15. Aikido Walking   132

16. Protecting the Attacker   144

17 The Wages of Optimism   153

18. The Primacy of Play   160

19. The Magical Marriage of Practice and Play   166

20. Under the Sword   180

21. The Beginner   189

Appendix: An Experiment in Human
    Transformation   195

Selected Readings   201

Acknowledgments   205

About the Author   207

CONTENTS

Introduction: A Revolutionary Martial Art   ix

1. Welcome to Our Dojo   1

2. Stepping on the Path   10

3. The First Life Lesson   16

4. "I Am the Universe"   26

5. The Centered Life   34

6. A Transformative Ordeal   48

7. Owning Your World   59

8. Adventure, Discovery, and a Dojo of Our Own   63

9. Context and Transformation   76

10. The Mysterious Power of *Ki*   83

11. Taking the Hit as a Gift   95

*This book is dedicated with love
to my grandchildren
Juliet & Adam Rubin
Brandon & Damon Sweetland
Bryan Leonard Fraim*

these grown-ups wearing exotic Japanese garb and exuberantly attacking one another, are dead serious in their concentration and, at the same time, having as much fun as children at play.

You wander over to a bulletin board covered with flyers of special events at this and other dojos. There in the middle is another, smaller photograph of the aged Japanese man and beneath it the words, "You should always practice in the spirit of joy." That quote helps you understand what's going on, but still there are mysteries. You look more closely at the photograph on the bulletin board, then back at the large one overlooking the training mat. You see a man from another era. His face is relatively unlined. His eyes are clear and calm. They are eyes that strike you as having seen more than most, not only of the material world but also of that vast interior universe that transcends ordinary time and space. They are eyes that hold you without asking anything of you. They are slightly distant, the eyes of a great warrior or a saint or, better—in a martial art built on paradox—a saintly warrior.

You return to your seat. The sensei who is teaching comes over to introduce himself and ask if you have any questions. You hardly know what to say but finally venture to inquire if the attacks are "real." The sensei smiles and assures you that they are real; punches aren't being pulled. But a hard strike doesn't *look* very hard, he explains, if instead of opposing it you move in and become one with it, even if only for a split second. When you do become one with the attack, *blend* with it, you create any number of options for yourself. And nobody gets hurt.

You ask about the venerable Japanese gentleman in the

photograph. The sensei explains that he was the founder of aikido. His name is Morihei Ueshiba, but he is known to aikidoists and to many practitioners of other martial arts, as well, simply as O Sensei, great teacher. When the picture was taken, he was just under five feet tall, weighed around a hundred and twenty pounds, and was at his prime as a martial artist. O Sensei, in fact, told his students that it was only after he had lost his muscular strength at age seventy and had to depend almost entirely on *ki* that he really understood the essence of aikido.

You want to ask about *ki*, but the sensei has to go and demonstrate the next phase of training. Before leaving, he tells you that you're welcome to come back any time you wish.

"The Greatest Martial Artist Who Ever Lived"

The practitioners of most martial arts derive inspiration from their founder, none more so than aikidoists. O Sensei was born in 1883 and died, at age eighty-six, in 1969. That was before I had even heard of aikido, so I never had the chance to meet him. My first teacher, however, trained with O Sensei in Japan and my present teacher apprenticed with him as *uchi deshi* (live-in student) for fifteen years. I've also met several other people who knew and studied with O Sensei, and whenever I and other aikidoists get together with these fortunate souls, we are prone to stay up late into the night, never tiring of the stories told and retold, tales of the founder's predilections, his eccentricities, his profound dedication to matters of the spirit, and of certain of his feats that challenge our secure faith in the impossible.

In his excellent biography, *Abundant Peace*, John Stevens offers an opinion of the founder's skill shared by almost all aikidoists and many practitioners of other arts as well. "Morihei was undoubtedly the greatest martial artist who ever lived. Even if we accept every exploit of all the legendary warriors, East and West, as being literally true, none of those accomplishments can be compared to Morihei's documented ability to disarm any attacker, throw a dozen men simultaneously, and down and pin opponents without touching them, recorded scores of times in photographs, on film, and by personal testimony."

Morihei Ueshiba was a hypersensitive, sickly, frail child. His father, a prosperous farmer and politician of samurai stock, encouraged him to build himself up by studying the martial arts. This was the beginning of a decades-long quest for physical power and the perfect martial art, a quest that would sweep Morihei up in enough adventures for several lifetimes. He studied the sword, staff, and spear, along with sumo wrestling and various forms of jujutsu. He took everything to extremes, strengthening his head by pounding it on a stone slab a hundred times a day, disappearing into the mountains for extended periods of fasting and other spiritual practices.

In his late twenties, after drifting from job to job and sensei to sensei, Morihei led a group of eighty-four people to start a new community in the frigid wilds of Hokkaido, Japan's Alaska. It was there that he met an old-time warrior named Sokaku Takeda, the master of Daito Ryu aikijutsu.

Sokaku was a grim and severe teacher who had killed a number of opponents in no-holds-barred duels. Nevertheless, Morihei was so impressed by his prowess that he gave himself totally to Sokaku, building a dojo and house for him on his own property and becoming, in effect, his servant so that he could receive instruction two hours a day. This difficult warrior continued following Morihei after he returned from Hokkaido. He was persuaded to leave only by an exorbitant "farewell gift" from Morihei. Still, Daito Ryu aikijutsu was to become a strong influence on the creation of O Sensei's aikido.

Never daunted in his quest, Morihei Ueshiba then gave himself heart and soul to another charismatic but questionable character, Onisaburo Deguchi, founder and guru of Omoto-Kyo, a cultlike religion that at one time had several million followers in Japan. In 1924, Onisaburo, Morihei, and a few other Omoto-Kyo followers left Japan bound on a secret expedition to the Chinese mainland. Their plan was to raise an army, foment a revolution, and take over Mongolia for Japan. After several battles, Onisaburo's group was captured, put in irons, and threatened with execution. The Chinese authorities, unwilling to provoke the Japanese government, finally issued a reprieve and the conspirators were released into the custody of the local Japanese consul.

Back in Japan, Morehei only intensified his physical training, his quest for spiritual enlightenment. Then, in the spring of 1925, at age forty-two, he experienced a life-changing vision. He had just finished a strenuous sword duel with a naval officer, during which it seemed he could see a beam of light showing him just where his opponent was going to strike next. He went to his garden, where he would draw water from the well to wash the sweat from his face and hands. Suddenly, he began to tremble and found it impossible to move. The earth seemed to shake and everything around him turned to gold—the well, the nearby persimmon tree, his own body. At that moment he heard the words, "I am the universe." All barriers between the material and spiritual worlds fell away, and Morihei was struck by the realization that the true destiny of the martial arts was not contention and domination but love.

Morihei Ueshiba's quest was not over; there would be more zigzags along the way. But he had found the basic course he would follow for the rest of his life. And this course would eventually lead to his revolutionary transfiguration of the martial arts. The Japanese term *jutsu* means "combat form," while *do* means "path" or "way of life." Aikijutsu, with its hard, linear movements, would evolve into aikido, with its flowing, circular movements. And aikido would become, in O Sensei's words, "not a technique to fight with or defeat the enemy. It is the way to reconcile the world and make human beings one family."

We Are Not Gods

O Sensei's life was filled with the kinds of episodes from which legends are made. Once, on his abortive expedition to Mongolia, he and his group were ambushed by Chinese soldiers. Facing a hail of bullets, Morihei discovered, according to his own account, that by remaining absolutely calm and concentrating *ki* in his mind and body, he could see "pebbles of white light flashing just before the bullets. I avoided them by twisting and turning my body." On another occasion, he was surrounded by men with knives. When they rushed at him, he seemingly disappeared, only to reappear on a flight of stairs some distance away.

A founder's miraculous feats are the bread and butter of the martial arts and are to be taken with a generous seasoning of salt. But those of O Sensei occurred in modern times and some of them are unique in having been recorded on film. After I had been doing aikido for only a few months, my first teacher brought in an 8mm projector so that after class we could sit on the mat and watch home movies of the founder in action.

And there he is, a somewhat frail-looking old man less than five feet tall with a wispy white beard and dressed in a long white robe. He is surrounded by several young martial artists holding wooden staffs. As they rush in to strike him, he "disappears" and the attackers collapse in a heap, revealing O Sensei smiling benignly on the other side of them. The flickering, slightly grainy black-and-white images somehow add to the authenticity of the action.

And then two attackers are converging on him from different directions at full speed. Just as they appear to reach him, he has inexplicably moved toward them, just past their lines of attack, and they have crashed together and he has pinned them to the mat, one on top of the other, holding the two of them down with one finger. My teacher reverses the film and plays this sequence over again slowly. Maybe there's something wrong with the film, but it does seem that

O Sensei has moved two or three feet and turned 180 degrees in what amounts to no time at all.

And then he is simply performing some of the standard techniques of aikido that we have practiced, except that he is moving with incomparable swiftness, grace, and ease. Attacked simultaneously by three muscular black belts, he sends them flying again and again, like chips from a woodcutter's ax.

I am sitting on the mat, still soaked with sweat, but the chill that runs up my spine has nothing to do with the temperature. I am aching with the daring of what I'm seeing, the beauty. Already, at this early stage of my aikido journey, I'm beginning to realize that aikido's philosophy rather than its physical techniques might well turn out to be of the greatest significance for the world. And I know I can never match the mastery that flickers on the small screen before me. But I will keep on practicing, not for prowess in self-defense, not for rank or prestige, not even for the wonderful and life-changing lessons that flow from this art. I will practice aikido for the sheer, unmitigated beauty of it.

CHAPTER 2

Stepping on the Path

It had all begun with a phone call. My close friend, Michael Murphy, co-founder of Esalen, a pioneering mind-body institute on the wild Big Sur coast of California, was more excited and enthusiastic than ever. Before I knew it, he was telling me about a martial art called aikido. He was saying that aikido was the most sophisticated of all systems of self-defense, that it had a rich and fascinating philosophy, that it promised certain spiritual insights. What's more, he had found an aikido teacher named Robert Nadeau who had studied in Japan with the founder of the art. He had decided to bring this teacher in to start an experimental aikido class for the staff of the San Francisco office of the institute he had started to see if this art should be added to the curriculum.

"The class will meet on Tuesdays and Thursdays from four to six," he said. "I'm inviting you to join the class. I'm going to do it. Let's go all the way to black belt, George. Let's do it!"

For a moment, I didn't know what to say. The idea of taking up a martial art had never crossed my mind. I had never heard of aikido. In fact, I had just reinstated my lapsed tennis club membership and had had to pay a rather hefty initiation fee for a second time. I was the kind of person who needed exercise to balance mental work and was facing an intense schedule of research and writing on a new book. How would I manage both tennis and aikido? Why ask? I knew from the beginning that I couldn't refuse Michael's enthusiastic invitation.

"Okay, Mike, let's do it," I said, having no idea that with those simple words I was stepping onto a path that would radically change my life.

An Unlikely Sensei

At first glance, you wouldn't think of Bob Nadeau as a martial artist. He was in his early thirties when I met him, a man of medium height and weight who wore glasses and dressed in a flashy, sometimes over the top manner. He came from a family of factory workers in upstate New York and didn't much care for bowing or other Eastern ceremonies; he used Japanese terms only when absolutely necessary. ("We're Yankees," he told us.) He had started judo at age fourteen, then karate and t'ai chi. At sixteen, he taught judo to police officers and later became a policeman himself. At the same time, he held a membership in a spiritual fellowship, read "metaphysical" books, and was a serious meditator. Even after studying with Morihei Ueshiba in Japan and getting his first black belt, he insisted he was primarily a meditation teacher. He spoke in a deep, resonant, and somewhat sardonic voice, stressing certain syllables in a way I'd never before encountered. ("Your technique was good e-*nough*, but it didn't make me *hap*-py.") He was always accompanied by his assistant, Betsy Hill, a slim, fine-boned young woman with long, straight, dark red hair and the face of an angel. Sometimes he brought one or two more senior students from his school forty-five miles south of San Francisco.

If Nadeau was an unlikely sensei, the fourteen of us who started out in the experimental class—office workers, group leaders, and some spouses—were even more unlikely candidates for the martial arts. One woman, a superb group leader, must have weighed 250 pounds. The man who headed the San Francisco office was fairly slim, but he seemed to have barely enough muscle tone to keep himself upright. Michael and I were in better shape than most, which wasn't all that great. We found a lovely place to hold our classes: a high-vaulted, octagonal chapel at San Francisco's Unitarian Center. Tall windows of colored glass captured the winter sun as it edged down toward the horizon, creating a warm, ever-changing interior light. We could move the folding chairs aside and cover the red tile floor with bright blue folding training mats held together snugly with Velcro.

Even in this ideal situation Nadeau was strangely reluctant to put the mats down and get on with the business of teaching us physical aikido. For a long time, this formidable martial artist had had a dream of teaching aikido principles to nonaikidoists. Now here he was with a group of "intellectuals" as students. What better opportunity to experiment with what he called "nonfalling aikido" or "energy awareness"?

He told us that we were "energy beings" and that we could extend our "energy legs" deep down into the earth to make ourselves more stable or our "energy arms" out beyond the horizon, thus creating incredible strength and resilience in our physical arms. We practiced making ourselves heavier so that it was practically impossible for anyone to lift us. We walked around and around, imagining that we were powered by a monorail that extended through our physical center of mass an inch or so beneath the navel. Standing still, we would rotate our bodies one way, then the other, letting our arms remain totally relaxed so that they would swing out then flop against us as we turned. We were asked to assume that *we* were not doing this exercise at all, but that *it* was doing it—*it* being some mysterious universal force, analogous perhaps to the impetus that "lets" the moon orbit the Earth and the Earth orbit the sun.

The Essence of Aikido

I didn't know at the time that these seemingly fanciful but often quite effective exercises would eventually play a part in my aikido practice and my workshops. I was fascinated, but I wanted—needed—some real exercise. "Come on, Bob," I would say. "Let's put the mats down." So we would bring out the mats and practice simple wrist locks or backward sit-falls, where we would roll over backward then come to a standing position. Once, to make a point, Nadeau motioned one of his aikido students to attack him. The student, a tall, rather ferocious-looking young man, rushed in to deliver a hard punch to his teacher's solar plexus. But Nadeau wasn't there to receive it. Almost faster than the eye could follow, he was at his student's side, somehow embracing him. Then there were two indescribable whirling motions that had the feeling of *sswwish* and *whooossh*, with the two bodies exchanging positions yet remaining perfectly linked, and suddenly the attacker was flying through the air, to land a few feet away with a loud slap of his hand on the mat. There was a moment of stunned silence, after which I said, "Would you please do that again?" Nadeau merely smiled and went on with his instruction.

After a couple of months, Nadeau started teaching us the aikido forward roll, not a straight, head-over-heels somersault, but a graceful, diagonal rotation, in which the body rolls from, say, the right hand, arm, and shoulder across the back to the left buttock and leg. Demonstrated by our teacher and his senior students, this maneuver, starting and ending in a standing position, seemed as effortless and serene as the turning of a large wheel. When our motley band tried it, however, the results resembled nothing so much as barely controlled crashes. Half the remaining students didn't show up for the next class.

Our fast-shrinking class kept meeting every Tuesday and Thursday. Martial arts traditionalists would have gnashed their teeth at our informality. There was no bowing. We called our teacher "Bob" rather than "sensei." There was still plenty of "energy awareness." But somehow, in halting steps, we began learning aikido, embodying such principles as moving from center, relaxing under pressure, and extending *ki* ("energy" in Nadeau's lexicon). And we began practicing the unique move that most sets aikido off from other forms of self-defense.

When confronted by any attack or problematic incoming energy, the aikidoist doesn't strike, push back, pull, or dodge, but rather *enters* and *blends*. That is, he or she moves *toward* the incoming energy and then, at the last instant, slightly off the line of attack, turning so as to look momentarily at the situation *from the attacker's viewpoint*. From this position, many possibilities exist, including a good chance of reconciliation.

Nadeau told us that the very essence of aikido is contained in the simplest blending move. He also told us that the blend could be used to good effect verbally as well as physically. He insisted, in fact, that everything he taught us could be applied to every aspect of our lives. "What you do with aikido off the mat," he said one day, "is really more important than what you do with it on the mat." I heard those words and nodded in agreement. But hearing something and agreeing with it is one thing. Changing lifelong habits is another. It took a hard jolt to awaken me to the truth of what he said and to convince me to start changing my ways.

CHAPTER 3

The First Life Lesson

I had been practicing aikido for three months, attending every class I could. At that time, I was averaging two out-of-town trips a month to give speeches based on my book, *Education and Ecstasy*, which had come out a couple of years earlier. The book had made a stir and my speeches were attracting large and spirited audiences, especially at colleges and universities. Most members of the audience came to support me or just to hear what I had to say, but there were always a few who were there to joust with the speaker.

My whole upbringing had taught me, as almost all of us are taught, that if I didn't win in such encounters I would lose, and that such an outcome would threaten not only my ideas but my authority as a speaker and writer, my very being. I knew from experience that every audience would probably include people armed with what they considered devastating objections to my proposals. What they hadn't stopped to consider, however, was that after two years' practice with this subject, I had not only worked out responses A, B, and C to every likely attack but had perfected my timing. I often used humor as a weapon, manipulating the audience to laugh at my detractor's expense. Though I might have gained some momentary satisfaction from my victories in these verbal jousts, they always left me feeling a little sick.

The episode that led to my awakening happened one night before an overflow audience in San Francisco. Ironically, I was speaking at the main sanctuary of the Unitarian Center, only a short distance from where we practiced aikido, which should have reminded me of my training. I spoke for about an hour then called for an intermission, which would be followed by a session devoted to questions from the audience.

As I walked into the lobby on the way to the men's room, I saw a group of people clustered around a stocky, red-faced man who was speaking in a loud voice and gesticulating angrily. When he saw me, he shouted, "Get over here, Leonard!" and motioned furiously for me to come to him. Even before I got there, he launched an attack. Not only would my proposals destroy our whole system of education, but they would also weaken the moral fiber of our nation.

I raised both hands in front of me as if holding him back. I told him I couldn't talk now but would recognize him first after the intermission. When I returned to the rostrum, I noticed him in the fifth or sixth row and to the right of me, his face still flushed. I gestured in his direction.

"I promised to recognize this gentleman first."

He was even more rabid than I had expected. I listened carefully, forcing myself to become cooler as his temperature continued to rise. When he had finished, I took a deep breath and began. Methodically, I sliced off an ear, then a hand, an arm, a shoulder. At the end, he was sitting down, slumping lower and lower in his seat, his face an even deeper red, as the entire audience howled with laughter at his expense.

I had won, and I was sick at heart.

I barely slept that night, and the next day, at work in my downtown office, I sensed something dark and noxious inside me. Was this the way life was supposed to be? Late that afternoon I received a special-delivery letter. "I'm the person you recognized first last night and I just want you to know how I felt when you finished with me. I felt humiliated, shamed, completely destroyed.   "

At that instant, like a cartoon light bulb over my head, the realization popped into my consciousness: I could have used aikido's entering and blending move *verbally*. I got up and began pacing around. Why hadn't I thought of it sooner? What an idiot I was. I could have blended and everything would have been different. And there were probably other aikido principles I could use during my speeches and actually—as my teacher had suggested—all the time.

Suddenly, I felt as if I had been released from some cramped dungeon into a vast landscape of possibilities. I sent off a conciliatory reply to my adversary and started looking forward to my next speech.

It was at a large midwestern university. The first questioner after my talk was an aggressive-looking young man with a wicked grin.

"That was a nice little scenario you gave us, but it's pure and unadulterated bullshit. Where would you get the money to pay for all that technology? The kind of computers you're talking about in your school of the future would cost more than the whole school building. This kind of futurism is ridiculous and irresponsible."

Previously, I might have responded with one of my pre-programmed verbal weapons, but this time I imagined myself down in the audience standing next to the young man, seeing things from his point of view. "That's a good question," I said. "I worry about that myself. What you're saying is that this new technology is very expensive."

"Yeah, right. And not only that, the computer capability you're talking about doesn't exist yet—and we're not even near getting there."

"Yeah, that's true, too."

My questioner paused. There was a change in the emotional climate.

"But you know," he said, "you know, computers keep getting cheaper all the time. And the increase in computer memory and speed is exponential."

"Right. I've heard that a generation in computer technology is now about three or four years."

"Well, maybe it could happen—if we had the will to do it."

"Right. If we had the will. Thanks very much for bringing it up."

He was smiling as he took his seat and I felt great. This bright young man had started out attacking. I had blended with his energy, seeing and acknowledging his point of view without giving up my own. And it had ended up with *him* making *my* point!

All that spring I traveled from audience to audience around the country in a state of bliss.

"I'm using aikido in my speeches," I told Nadeau.

"Good," he said. My teacher was not one to waste his breath on superfluous plaudits.

There was another small miracle in June of that year. It happened in Tulsa, where I was addressing a luncheon meeting of the Oklahoma Education Association. As usual, I asked for questions or comments after finishing my prepared speech. The exchange went on and on, longer than ever before, and still I kept milking the audience for questions. People started looking at their watches. I knew I should end it—these educators had to go back to work—but something seemed to be missing; I just couldn't bring to mind what it was. Then it hit me.

"Doesn't anybody have a hostile question?" I laughingly asked.

The educators looked around at one another and shrugged. I searched the room for any signs of attack. There were none.

In all the years since then, during hundreds of appearances, I've never had a hostile question from an audience at a speech, not even once. I often ask myself how this can be. I'm fairly certain I haven't censored myself or weakened my message in any way. Maybe it's just that by being prepared to blend I don't have to.

The small miracles that resulted from this use of aikido were the first of many. I was to learn that the aikido philosophy translates easily into surprisingly effective guidelines for living.

The Art of Verbal Blending

What do you do when somebody pushes you?

Over the past twenty-five years, I've posed this question to groups totaling more than fifty thousand people in workshop sessions, and the first answer in every case has been "Push back." I've heard "Push back," as a matter of fact, in four languages: English, French, German, and Spanish. From this experience, I've concluded that the practice of pushing back whenever pushed is ubiquitous in Western culture—and, I suspect, in other cultures as well.

And here, of course, we're not just talking about a physical push. It's unlikely you'll be pushed physically between now and this time next week. But the odds are pretty good that someone will push you verbally or psychologically. And if you're like most people, you're quite likely to push back verbally or psychologically. So let's see what options you have, what outcomes you can expect, in case you do. It's simple: You can win, you can lose, or there can be a stalemate—none of which is conducive to harmony and mutual satisfaction. If you win, somebody else has to lose. If you lose, it doesn't feel very good. And a stalemate's a big waste of time.

It could be said that the health of an individual or an organization is generally directly proportionate to the number of perceived options at its command. The converse is also true. When an individual or an organization moves toward breakdown, that move is generally accompanied by the perception of fewer and fewer options. Isn't it strange, then, that when we're being pushed, we've limited ourselves to a response that results in only three options, none of them particularly good?

What's the alternative? To deal with any kind of push, whether a shove or strike or kick, the aikidoist generally moves toward the attacker and slightly off the line of attack, simultaneously making a turning maneuver that leaves him or her next to the attacker and facing in the same direction. In this position, the aikidoist is looking at the situation *from the attacker's viewpoint*. It's important here to add one more phrase to that statement. The aikidoist is looking at the situation from the attacker's viewpoint *without giving up his or her own viewpoint*.

This *entering* and *blending* maneuver immediately multiplies your options. Thousands of techniques and variations have been identified in aikido, all of which become possible once you've blended. The same thing is true when you blend verbally, when instead of meeting a verbal attack with a verbal counterattack you respond first by coming around to your attacker's point of view, seeing the situation from his or her viewpoint. This response, whether physical or verbal, is quite disarming, leaving the attacker with no target to focus on. At that point, numerous options present themselves, including, best of all, the clear possibility of a reconciliation that meets the needs of both parties.

This isn't to say that we should always blend. In some cases, pushing back, standing your ground, and striking out forcefully is necessary or appropriate. It would have been difficult, probably impossible, to blend with Hitler. Diplomats of the 1930s tried and failed. But we could also say that, in trying to appease the dictator, the Western democracies failed to maintain their own points of view, which is essential to the successful practice of this option. In any case, blending isn't the answer for every situation; it's a means by which you can multiply your options in responding to any kind of attack.

Then, too, it's possible to strike effectively *after* blending. In physical aikido, as a matter of fact, a successful blend almost always creates an opening for a throw or a pin.

Yes, sometimes I fail to blend when I should have blended, and I'm almost always sorry for it. Radio talk shows offer a marvelous opportunity to practice this skill and sometimes, just as a reminder, I write the word BLEND in large letters on a card placed near the microphone. Again and again blending and other skills learned in aikido have produced outcomes that would seem unlikely if not miraculous, as we'll see later. For now, let me sum up with a few guidelines on the art of blending.

Blend from a grounded and centered stance. Whether the attack is physical or verbal, it's important that you be firmly connected to the earth with your energy concentrated in your "center," or *hara* (the Japanese word for belly), as you blend. It's difficult to blend with your energy concentrated in your head, shoulders, or chest. Since energy follows attention, put your attention on the soles of your feet and on a point an inch or two below your navel. You might touch this point as a reminder. If you receive a verbal attack while seated, put your attention on your buttocks and the small of your back as well as on the soles of your feet. Sink into the chair. Feel the small of your back on the backrest. Let your shoulders remain relaxed and supple and make sure your breath doesn't rise into your upper chest. Let your breath expand your *hara*, and if the attack is verbal, speak slowly and with genuine feeling as you respond.

Don't overblend. Responding to a verbal attack by saying something on the order of "Yes, you're right and I'm wrong and I'm a bad person" isn't blending. By saying anything along the lines of "I'm a bad person," you bring the attention back to yourself rather than truly looking at the situation from the attacker's viewpoint. Stay grounded and centered. Honor your own viewpoint *while* seeing the situation from your attacker's viewpoint. Sometimes a blend involves an apology, but blending isn't just giving in or denigrating yourself. It's seeking harmony through a reconciliation that honors *both* viewpoints.

Avoid the overuse of blending with your mate, family, and close friends Blending is extremely powerful. Using it all the time can drive people close to you crazy. There are times when people want to and need to grapple with one another verbally, to have an old-fashioned give-and-take. Again, let me stress that blending is a valuable and often surprisingly effective option, but it isn't the only way to deal with incoming energy.

If you're going to blend, do it wholeheartedly. The inadequacy of a less-than-wholehearted physical blend is dramatically revealed in aikido. When an aikidoist makes a halfhearted attempt at blending while hurrying to pull off a technique, the technique is almost sure to fail. The same thing is true in verbal blending. The blend isn't just a trick with which to fool an adversary. It involves true understanding of the other person's intentions and feelings. Ideally, a verbal blend conveys this understanding. It involves empathy. It comes from the heart.

Practice! Blending is one of those rare skills that sometimes produces immediate good results. But to blend consistently and to do so under pressure requires a great deal of practice. Start simply by listening carefully and sympathetically to *everything* people say to you. (Remember, this doesn't necessarily mean agreeing.) When you get really good at this, you might be surprised at how successfully you can blend under pressure. After attending one of my weekend workshops that stressed blending, a leading San Francisco public advocacy lawyer was opposed by eleven corporate lawyers in a meeting with a judge in chambers. "I decided to see if this stuff works," he told me later. "I blended with everything they said for an hour, after which they conceded to my point."

Realize that harmony can spring from the meeting of opposites. To blend is to move toward the attack, creating a dance that joins attacker and defender and opens the way to reconciliation. It yields reliable good results, but it really isn't about winning. Blending is an expression of love, of a willingness to embrace even the strongest attack and bring it into a circle of concord that somehow connects each individual to the essential unity and harmony of the universe.

CHAPTER 4

"I Am the Universe"

The experimental class dwindled until there were only two of us, myself and my friend Leo Litwak, who had given up a career as a philosophy teacher to teach and write fiction. Leo and I never missed a class unless we were out of town. We drove in together, never tiring of our discussions about aikido—as self-defense, as art, as philosophy. We enjoyed a spectacular teacher-student ratio: Nadeau always brought Betsy Hill and at least one other senior student with him to train with us. After a year the experimental class was closed down. But no matter. Nadeau had started an evening class on Tuesdays and Thursdays from seven to nine that was open to the public. He had the mats and was already there, so why not? Reluctant to lose our privileged position, we joined the public class.

By then, we had learned enough of *kihon waza* (basic techniques) to have been awarded blue belts, one small step up from the white belt that marks the brand-new beginner. This made us the most advanced students on the mat, and also, in a sense, the most inexperienced. We had become accustomed to the precise attacks and smooth techniques of Nadeau and his senior students. And now what a change! This urban center attracted a kaleidoscopic and sometimes dreamlike clientele: street people, unemployed rock musicians, ferocious jocks, stoned hippies, recently divorced men and women with hungry eyes. Instructed to attack with a blow to the solar plexus, a new student—malicious or just disoriented—would try to kick me in the shins. On one occasion, a woman trying out the class was so drunk or drugged that when told to walk up and grab my wrist, she could never locate it. What could I do? I went over and put my wrist in her grasp and carefully led her off the mat and to a chair. After a few months, I began to think that nothing could surprise me. During that segment of my aikido journey, I found myself silently repeating a favorite samurai chant: *Expect nothing. Be ready for anything.*

Actually, it was wonderful training. And it deepened the mysteries that surround and permeate all martial arts, especially aikido: Why should people try to hurt or kill one another in the first place? If attacks of any kind come, how are we to deal with them? How can we protect our attackers? How can we help to end all hurtful conflict?

And the even deeper mystery: How are we to live?

O Sensei's Obsession

Gradually, the fringes faded away and a group of serious aikido students coalesced, enough so that Nadeau and two black-belt colleagues were emboldened to open a large dojo in San Francisco. But the mysteries remained. It was as if the more I knew about aikido, the less I knew. At one point, Nadeau told us that a Japanese admiral had tried to list all possible aikido techniques and variations and had come up with some ten thousand. But there are more. In fact, if you consider every conceivable variation, and also every counter, and every counter to a counter, the number of possibilities is infinite. And it could be said that these physical techniques, as beautiful as they might be, are only the surface manifestations of a more profound reality. Yet there are certain moments of physical beauty, just as there are certain combinations of words, which create a vibrancy that seems to strike straight down to the core of existence. Take the words that O Sensei heard during his life-changing vision of 1925:

"I am the universe."

Again and again he repeated these words. Even his close students were sometimes baffled. How could O Sensei liken himself to all of existence?

"When an enemy tries to fight with me, the universe itself," he later said, "he has to break the harmony of the universe. Hence, at the moment he has the mind to fight with me, he is already defeated. There exists no measure of time—fast or slow."

However strange these words might seem, the experiences of martial artists who have had the privilege of serving as his attackers during demonstrations seem to verify the founder's words. Robert Nadeau went to Japan in 1963 to study judo, karate, t'ai chi, and aikido but soon discovered in aikido's founder all the legendary powers he had been seeking. The first time he was allowed to attack Morihei was a revelation. "With all my years of training in the martial arts, I wanted to show him what I had, so I really came in hard. But when I got close to him, it was like I had entered a cloud. And in the cloud there was something like a giant spring that first compressed then turned me around and threw me out. I found myself flying through the air and came down with a hard, judo-style slap-fall. Lying there, I looked everywhere for O Sensei, but he wasn't to be seen. Finally I turned all the way around, the one place I wouldn't have expected him to be, and there he was, standing calmly."

Mitsugi Saotome, a master teacher who now lives in the United States, my own present teacher, tells of one of the countless times he was called upon to attack O Sensei. There was a shattering *ki-ai* cry from the founder and Saotome found himself being sucked "deep into the vacuum of a black hole from which there was no escape. Deep within my core a bomb exploded, and the whole universe expanded. There was nothing but light, blinding, searing light, and energy. I could not see or feel my body and the only reality was the enormous energy expanding from it. For those watching, it happened in the split of a second, but for me time had stopped. There was no time, no space, no sound, no color, and the silence was more deafening than his scream. In the light so completely, I *was* the light, and my mind and spirit were illuminated and completely clear. Then I was unconscious. As my body connected with the tatami mat, I was revived."

Morihei told Saotome, "My energy, my power, is not controlled by me. I am empty, but through my body flows the energies of the universe. My power is not my power. It is the universal power." And later he said, "Aikido will come to completion when each individual, following his or her true path, becomes one with the universe."

A questionable path for those of us swayed by the fashionable pessimism of these times. There is that familiar formulation, passed along uncritically from writer to writer, about how the human individual has been successively reduced and dethroned by the discoveries of Western science—removed from his honored place in the center of the heavenly bodies by Copernicus and others, removed from his position as lord and master of the animal kingdom by Darwin, removed even from command of his own acts by Freud and the behaviorists.

This notion of dethronement holds up, however, only if we consider ourselves previously enthroned in such simplistic and linear ways. Yes, I am small. The universe is 10^{26} times larger than I am. But my consciousness—and yours—can embrace the entire universe. "A small galaxy only a few light-years across" is an idea we can easily envelop. Yes, I consider myself part of a long developmental line, descended from creatures resembling monkeys or apes, rather than the product of a special, onetime creation. But I see the evolutionary journey as powerful evidence of God's work to create ever-higher levels of spirit from matter, a journey of spine-tingling eloquence and grandeur, the story of all stories.

And yes, my mind—and yours—has depths and heights beyond our conscious awareness and moment-by-moment control. But would we want it any other way? Ambiguity, the Argentine author, Jorge Luis Borges, reminds us, is a richness. Our brain, much less our mind, is forever unknowable, our ultimate creative capacity, for all practical purposes, infinite. The human brain is, in fact, the most complex, highly organized entity in the known universe. Each of us contains, and transcends, every form of matter that has come together since time began: quarks, electrons, protons, neutrons, atoms, molecules, cells, organelles, organs, organ systems, and finally the mysterious organization of all of this into self-aware consciousness itself. We stand at a vanguard, so far as we now know, of the universe's journey of adventure and discovery. An archaeologist of evolution could discover within each of us a full record of that incredible journey.

Each of us, then, can be viewed as a context of the entire universe from a particular point of view. To say it more simply, each of us *is* the universe from a particular point of view.

But Morihei Ueshiba, O Sensei, founder of aikido, has already said it: "I am the universe."

And so is everybody else.

Saying it is one thing. Experiencing it as O Sensei did, so fully, so deeply that the power of the universe flows through you, is another. Few of us have the opportunity or the will to travel Morihei's lifelong path of devotion and practice, but every one of us can begin, and perhaps in that beginning sense a shift in the climate of our own lives.

Becoming the Universe: A Beginning

Imagine yourself in an open area, a grassy hill far removed from city lights, on a clear, moonless night. Arching above you is an immense crystalline dome of air, a giant lens through which to view the universe. Lie on the grass and behold the stars in all their sparkling clarity and the Milky Way, that lustrous cloud of stars in which our sun has found its home, and beyond that stars without number.

But wait. Some of what you take to be stars are not stars at all but distant galaxies containing billions of stars and perhaps harboring intelligent life. And if you are looking at a galaxy (some of the nearer ones have the appearance of slightly fuzzy stars), you can be sure that it is moving directly away from you. The one high above is moving away from you. The one on the western horizon is moving away from you and so is the one to the east. And if you could look straight down through the body of the Earth, the galaxies you would see there are also moving directly away from you.

A marvel: In an expanding universe, every point in open space acts as if it is the center of the universe. There is no up, no down, no known circumference, only centers everywhere. This means that, in a sense, our galaxy *is* the center of the universe.

And so is every other galaxy.

Let's say, then, that each of us can act as if we are located in the center of existence—allowing all others the same privilege. This offers us the opportunity to connect our own center with the center of the universe. To do so, however, we must get truly in touch with our *own* center. To begin experiencing the self and the universe as one, we must learn to sit, stand, move, speak, feel, think, create, and love as if the impetus for each of these activities arises in our center of mass, a point in the middle of the abdomen an inch or so beneath the navel.

Thus, we have come to the matter of *centering:* an art, a science, a practice, a way of being in the world that is fundamental to everything in this book.

CHAPTER 5

The Centered Life

Y ou do aikido," my new friend says. "Have you ever, you know, used it?"

"Oh, I use it all the time—when I'm walking, when I'm playing the piano, when—"

"What I mean is, have you ever   had to   *use* it?"

It's the kind of question aikidoists get all the time. And no wonder. What with all the choreographed violence in martial arts movies and video games, it's hard to explain that the ultimate purpose of every responsible martial art is to reduce violence, to make fighting unnecessary. Sometimes, of course, violent attacks do occur, and there are cases where aikido training has been used to subdue that violence. But, for the aikidoist, the best stories involve practitioners who have prevented the outbreak of violence or stopped violence already under way. How did they do it? In certain cases, it was by something you, too, might do—something as simple as *centering*, that is, putting your attention on your physical center of mass, a point in the abdomen about an inch or two beneath the navel.

Tales of Centering

After some two years of training, Jonathan had achieved blue-belt rank in aikido. He was also a dedicated Zen student and was living at the San Francisco Zen Center. Walking back to the center late one night, he paid little attention to the two young men coming toward him on the sidewalk. When they came close, they split up, one on either side of him. He heard a sharp click and saw the glint of a streetlight on metal as the man on the left drew a switchblade.

"I didn't know what to do," Jonathan told me, "so I just centered. I stood there and they stood there. At that point, I figured, Well, I'm already here, so I might as well stay here. I was in *hanmi* [a balanced stance with one foot ahead of the other, the back foot turned out about forty-five degrees]. My hands were by my sides and all I was concentrating on was my center."

The three of them stood there for what seemed a long time but might have been only seconds. Then the man on the left said, "Guess we got the wrong man." He closed his switchblade, nodded to his companion, and the two of them continued on their way.

Ed was an airline pilot flying 727s on the San Francisco–Boston route. He held a first-degree black belt in aikido. One night he was walking through Boston's combat zone (clearly not the best part of town) when a young woman ran toward him, obviously in great distress.

"Please help me," she cried. "Somebody's beating up my girlfriend."

He followed her, and there, right around the corner, was a small group watching a man holding a woman by her hair, slapping her, shaking her, and otherwise roughing her up. Ed walked up close to the man but not too close, took a *hanmi* stance, and centered. He didn't say a word—no threats, no pleas, no reasoning—nor did he assume any of the exotic fighting poses you see in martial arts movies. He just stood there calmly, hands by his sides, and concentrated on his center.

"The man looked at me," Ed said, "then turned back to the woman. He looked at me again, then turned back again to the woman. The third time he looked at me, he let her go and ran as fast as he could."

If these episodes seem fanciful or magical, there are studies that show a strong correlation between the way people walk or stand and the likelihood of their being physically attacked. At Rahway State Prison in New Jersey, convicted muggers were shown videotapes of people walking on New York City sidewalks and asked which ones they would have mugged during their criminal careers. In most cases, the muggers were in complete agreement with one another. The people they would have picked as victims were not necessarily the smallest or weakest-looking, but rather those who were in some way out of balance, out of sync. Those walking in a balanced and centered manner were hardly ever chosen as potential victims.

It's possible, but not easy, to exaggerate the power of centering. One reason we don't readily credit the power of this way of being is that it is rarely if ever modeled in the popular entertainment that increasingly dominates our lives. Instead, we are treated to episodes without end of uncentered behavior, scores of them during an average week of television. It's easy, if trivializing, for actors to propel the action by screaming, cursing, threatening, taunting, shoving, striking, shooting, and blowing things up. One well-known film director was reported as saying that when nothing much seems to be happening, you can always put in another explosion. But explosions, whether chemical or human, produce nothing so much as the demand for bigger and more spectacular explosions, an escalation that eventually numbs the senses and leads to despair. It takes courage and will to explore the drama that underlies every moment of every life and to show the subtle and ultimately definitive power of a way of being that leads toward greater harmony.

Getting Centered

At first, it seems ridiculously simple: All you have to do is put your attention on the center of your abdomen (*hara* in Japanese), at a point one inch or two below the navel, and things will be better in many ways. This is true and it is rather simple and you get immediate results. But the matter of centering has ramifications that could take a lifetime to play out. There is centering in stillness and centering in rapid motion. There is centering under pressure and centering while in pain. There is regaining center after disorientation or defeat and remaining centered during moments of great triumph. There is centered driving and flying and horseback riding and skiing and every other sport. There is centered talking and centered lovemaking. And while physical centering is always a prerequisite, there is also centering in such nonphysical activities as research, writing, art, philosophy, science. And there are centered families, teams, organizations, and cultures.

The problem is that most of us don't start out putting much attention on our physical centers. When asked where their "I" is located, most people would say "In my head," which seems logical enough. After all, your brain, nose, mouth, eyes, and ears are located in that part of your body. Logic is always important, but it is also always partial, as it is based on a one-to-one physical and symbolic correspondence that doesn't exist in the real world. When the aikidoist is told to "see from your *hara*," he or she, of course, doesn't try to make eyes appear in the center of the belly, but rather becomes highly aware of the center and the connection between it and the eyes. "When seeing from the center," the aikido student is far more successful in dealing with attacks, especially multiple attacks, than when seeing with the eyes alone. To see from the center, breathe from the center, and move from the center leads us to a sense that the locus of our very being is centered in the *hara*. And this sense, this feeling, this practice can change our lives.

When asked "What area of the body do you associate with physical strength?" many people, especially men, would say, "The upper chest, shoulders, and arms." Movies and television dramas often show just that part of the body, with muscles tensed, to signify male strength. ("These are my guns," one character said, displaying his pumped-up biceps.)

This answer, however, is totally off the mark. The long muscles—thigh, buttocks, abdomen, back—that attach to the pelvic girdle are far stronger than the macho muscles of upper chest, shoulders, and arms. Even such actions as striking and throwing derive most of their power from muscles below the waist. Physically as well as symbolically, the *hara* can be treated as the center of power.

The physical advantages of centering can be easily demonstrated. Sit on a bench or in a straight-backed chair, hands in your lap, feet a foot or so apart on the floor. Have a friend stand behind you. Practice standing up from this seated position several times, not using your hands to help push you up. Then have your friend put his or her hands on your shoulders and exert a reasonable amount of downward pressure, perhaps just enough to keep you from standing up. Put your attention on your shoulders and on the hands that are holding you down. Try to stand up. You might not be able to stand at all. If you do manage to get up, notice how much effort it took.

Be seated again. Relax. Breathe from center. Put your attention on your center. Briefly touch your center. Then have your friend put his hands on your shoulders and exert exactly the same amount of downward pressure as before. This time it's your center that's going to be rising. Don't be concerned about your shoulders; when your center rises, they will, too. Concentrate on that point in the center of your abdomen from which the action will come. Consider the possibility that the impulse to rise comes from there.

Note the difference between the two ways of rising from a seated position. Discuss it with your friend.

You can also check to see how well a centered stance affects your ability to stay balanced under pressure. Stand with your feet about shoulder-width apart and have your friend stand at your side, facing you. Bring your attention to your head, say, at a point in the center of your forehead. Briefly touch that point. Have your friend place the palm of his or her hand on your upper back and push you forward, starting lightly and then gradually adding pressure until you have to step forward with one foot to regain your balance.

Pause, breathe deeply from center, and take the same stance you did before. This time, place your attention at your center and feel the soles of your feet firmly planted on the floor. Touch your center briefly. Have your friend push you forward again, exactly as he or she did the first time. Note the difference, not just whether you could stay balanced without stepping forward, but also how you *felt* during the experiment. Again, discuss it with your friend.

There are many ways of checking the difference between the uncentered state and the centered one. You might say that all of aikido is an experiment of this sort, conducted at times under extreme pressure. And the difference between the two states, centered and uncentered, becomes more and more apparent as the pressure increases.

But you don't need to take up a martial art to enjoy the benefits and pleasures of being centered. You can practice centering every time you take a walk, even when you stroll from one room to another in your house. Think of it. Pay close attention to your every step, the swing of your arms, the tilt of your head. You are walking with full awareness of your center as it moves powerfully and effortlessly through space. You are breathing easily down into your *hara*. Your shoulders, neck, chest, and abdomen are relaxed. Your legs are swinging in perfect counterpoise with your arms. Your hips, too, are engaged in this elemental rhythm, and you are deliciously aware of the soles of your feet blending with the surface beneath them.

Body and Mind Reunited

In times past, and even now wherever the Victorian age has lingered, body and mind have been seen not only as separate but as in constant conflict, the rebellious body driven by sensuous, irrational desires, the imperial mind sensible and censorious. Such a view is becoming more and more difficult to maintain. As our understanding of human thought and behavior increases, we can see that what we call "mind" and what we call "body" reflect and influence each other with amazing fidelity. Think of someone you know who is habitually ahead of himself physically, someone who stands and walks with head and shoulders thrust forward. In most cases, you'll find that such a person also tends to be ahead of himself in purely mental activities, even in something as intellectual as writing a technical or scholarly paper, jumping to conclusions without bringing up adequate background and supporting material.

In the same way, a person who, to say it inelegantly, habitually drags his butt physically is likely to show the same tendency verbally, producing written reports that take what seems forever to get to the point. Once, when nothing much was happening in the first two pages of a story I was reading to my then five-year-old daughter, she said, "But, Daddy, where's the bear?" Reading grown-up material from a butt-dragging writer, I, too, am often tempted to plead, "For God's sake, bring on the bear."

Centering affects the outcome of your actions in many ways. To go into a tense, adversarial situation, perhaps a business meeting, with body awareness concentrated in head, shoulders, and upper chest is almost certain to produce a different outcome than would be the case if you went into the same situation with attention on the *hara*. The former is more likely to lead to feelings of tension, a heated, ineffectual exchange of words, perhaps an escalation of the conflict, while the latter tends to bring calm confidence and the possibility of reconciliation. Numerous workshops and training sessions for businesspeople are currently available. Some of them are quite good in suggesting more effective ways of communication and various verbal formulas for success, but without a commensurate attention to bodily states, good results are problematical.

To check out the effect of centering on goal achievement, you might try an exercise I call "Three Ways of Reaching a Goal." In this exercise, you'll need a clear, level space of at least twenty feet and a friend to help you out. Stand at one side of this space facing the other side. Imagine that behind you is your home with all its comforts. To achieve your goal, you must leave your home and walk to a spot at least twenty feet in front of you. Your friend stands at your side, facing you, and gives instructions:

"Let's say achieving your goal involves walking over there to the other side of the room. Let's say it's a worthwhile goal. To reach it, you're going to have to overcome an obstacle. You're going to try it three ways, and for each way you should walk at a medium-fast pace—*exactly the same speed all three times* The first way, as you're walking toward your goal, you'll be thinking, Gosh, I wish I were home in bed. Your center of awareness and energy will be the back of your head."

Your friend gently taps the back of your head and snaps his or her fingers behind your head to draw your attention to that point. He or she walks to a spot halfway to your goal and extends an arm to block your way. The arm should be at shoulder level, below the level of the neck and above the level of the breast. Once your friend is set, you begin to walk toward the goal. Your friend gives you a medium amount of resistance. *It should be the same amount all three times*

After your first attempt to reach the goal, both you and your friend go back to the starting point and your friend again instructs you:

"All right, there's your goal and it's a worthwhile goal. This time, I don't want you to think about anything except getting there. Score the touchdown. I don't care how you score it. Scoring is all that counts. Sell the ad. I don't want to know how you sold the ad. This time, your center of awareness and energy will be in your forehead."

Your friend gently taps your forehead and snaps his or her fingers in front of your forehead to draw your attention to that point. He or she then takes the same position as before to play the part of the obstacle and provides the same amount of resistance. Note the difference both in outcome and feelings between the first and second ways.

After this attempt, both you and your friend go back to the starting point and your friend once again instructs you:

"Okay, there's your goal and it's a worthwhile goal. This time, as you're going to your goal, I want you to be aware of everything that's happening, every step of the way. As you're going to your goal, you'll be aware of the soles of your feet on the surface beneath them and you'll be saying to yourself, 'I'm here, I'm here, *and* I'm going to my goal.' Your center of awareness and attention is the center of your abdomen, an inch or two beneath your navel. Be sure to walk at the same speed as you did before."

Your friend gently taps your physical center and snaps his or her fingers in front of it to draw your attention to that point. He or she then provides the same amount of resistance as on the previous attempts. Note the difference between this third way and the previous two ways of reaching a goal.

I've presented this exercise to thousands of people, an overwhelming majority of whom have found the third way to be the most effective by far. With attention focused on the back of the head and on the comfortable home they've left behind, people tend to be easily stopped. With attention on the forehead and on the goal alone, they sometimes overcome the obstacle and reach their goal, but there's generally something unpleasant and jerky about their struggle with the obstacle. Moving from center while paying attention to both the goal and the path to the goal, thus staying in the present moment, produces a feeling of flow and ease that translates into seemingly effortless power. Those people acting as obstacles are often startled. To experience truly centered power sometimes takes their breath away. In aikido, the word *power* doesn't denote power over others. We go back to the word's French and Latin roots, meaning "to be able." It refers to your *ableness* to realize your potential, to fulfill, in O Sensei's words, "your bestowed mission on this planet."

Consider the possibility of applying this easy, flowing power to your quest for the most important goals of your life.

Joining the Center of the Universe

For the most part thus far, I've offered examples of the benefits of centering in practical, physical terms. But while it might start in the body, centering radiates out to every aspect of human existence. As I've pointed out, it affects how we think and feel, how we drive our cars, how we do our jobs, how we make love, how we relate to the realm of spirit. Today, when so many of us seek personal identity through what we buy, what car we drive, what corporate logo we wear on our clothes, what television shows we watch, centering returns us to our true selves, liberating us from the tyranny of passing fads and providing a stable place from which to perceive and act.

Centering rejoins our disordered parts. At the height of the sexual revolution of the 1970s, millions of people let themselves be swept up in an activity called "recreational sex." In doing so, they created an uncentered and precarious alliance between the genitals and the head, totally bypassing the heart and center. A return to center yields rich rewards: a full-bodied love that involves not only heart but also soul.

The breathless, uncentered seeker, energy concentrated in the eyes and top of the head, is fair game for every authoritarian guru, every religious scam. Giggling approvingly at the guru's most nonsensical pronouncements, the seeker plays follow-the-leader with glazed eyes, even to the point of death. Centering rejoins heaven and earth, returning the seeker to that personal autonomy requisite for any authentic relationship with the divine.

The angry person, energy concentrated in eyes, jaw, throat, arms, shoulders, and chest, is a self-destructive trigger waiting to be pulled. Breathing deep into the *hara* relieves the tension in the upper body and starts to bring the deranged parts of the being into harmony, preventing verbal or physical violence to others—or to himself or herself.

Centering is the foundation of aikido practice and philosophy. To be centered is to say yes to life. The center joins past and future, heaven and earth, the near and the far, the way out and the way in. It is a secure place from which to venture forth and to which you can always return. And if you want to know what O Sensei meant when he said, "I am the universe," you must first find and inhabit your own physical center, then, through meditation or intense concentration, in stillness and in action, feel it as one with the center of the universe—your center and the center of the universe one and the same.

Could it be that it is the place you already inhabit?

CHAPTER 6

A Transformative Ordeal

By the end of my third year of practicing aikido, I was regularly using exercises derived from my training with Nadeau in workshop sessions for nonaikidoists throughout the United States and overseas. More than ever I was convinced that the philosophy of aikido has something valuable to offer every man, woman, and child on this planet: increased options, positive changes of context, a practical understanding of the power of love, and finally a spiritual path toward personal and world peace.

But isn't the actual practice of aikido necessary for an understanding of its philosophy? Valuable, yes, but not necessary. And physical aikido obviously isn't for everyone. Even world-class athletes must be willing to endure periods of clumsiness, and the words *mastering aikido* constitute a self-canceling phrase. Analyzing the physics of aikido in *Scientific American*, Jearl Walker concluded that "it is the most difficult of all the martial arts to learn. Its demands for skill, grace, and timing rival those of classical ballet." There are no *kata* (movements performed alone in a certain sequence); you need a partner with whom you can take turns playing the part of attacker. Size and strength don't count as much as your ability to tune in to your attackers' intentions and momentum, then move in just such a way as to become one with them. Men and women, young and old, all practice together. Still, considerable stamina is required to take the falls and to get up off the mat hundreds of times in a two-hour class.

Then there's the matter of injuries. As is said about football, God must not have been thinking about aikido when He made the human knee. And learning to recover with a graceful roll after being thrown through the air is joyful and impressive—unless you should come unhinged while aloft. During my second year in the art, I suffered a shoulder separation, then, about a year later, a dislocation of the same shoulder. With all this, along with the usual aches of strenuous physical activity, my fitness level continued to improve.

Knowing that practicing hurt is part of the aikido scene, I wasn't at first worried when my friend Leo came up with a bothersome pain in his left knee. He went on practicing, but less frequently than usual. He was carrying a heavy schedule of teaching writing at his university and was having trouble with a novel of his own. But I couldn't believe he would cease training for good. I was wrong. Not long after the two of us received brown belts (the next belt below black), I knew he wasn't coming back. Out of our original class, I was the only one left. This was undoubtedly due to the fact that we had been enlisted as a group, without regard for individual fitness, aptitude, or motivation. But even among the self-selected, the dropout rate was considerable. What was needed, it seemed, was a systematic way to introduce the beginner to this formidable art in a gradual and gentle way.

A few months after Leo left, Nadeau called four of us who had persevered, three men and one woman, all brown belts, into the office and told us he was initiating hour-long fundamentals classes for new students, to be held three times a week before the regular evening sessions. He wanted us to teach the class. We took to our assignment with more avidity than we were willing to admit, planning our classes carefully, giving one another feedback on our teaching techniques. After having been beginners for so long, we loved having the keys to the dojo. It was even all right that Nadeau sometimes referred to us as the Four Fundamentalists.

We had been teaching for nearly a year when he suggested that we drive to another city and witness a black-belt exam. Spectators ringed the mat. Students in their *gi* knelt along the edges. An examining board of five ranking black belts from various dojos sat in judgment at one end. I joined a crowd clustered along the railing of a balcony overlooking the scene. The event hadn't yet begun. There were hushed voices, smiles of greeting for latecomers. It was like being at a wedding just before the music begins.

The host sensei clapped his hands and led all the aiki-doists on the mat in a deep bow. The first candidate flowed through his techniques without a false move. During the climactic all-out, three-person attack, the *randori*, he easily eluded his attackers and sent them flying, as the spectators gasped and applauded. Before the exams, I had wondered if the attackers would come in with real intent. My doubts were put to rest. I was impressed by the speed and abandon of the attacks.

After a short intermission, the second candidate, a stocky, tough-looking man in his early thirties, came to the center of the mat with his *uke* (attacker). Right away I could tell something was wrong. The man's movements were rough and uncertain. As the attacks intensified, his blending movements were becoming incomplete or entirely absent. Things went from bad to worse; the exam was endless, one of those nightmares in which you seem to be struggling through mud. Time came for the *randori*, and the attackers roared in, hard and clean and true. Again and again the failing candidate was nailed. He took a hard blow to the belly, a chop to the neck. Twice he went down.

I was awestruck. Driving home, I tried to sort out my feelings about this art, which now seemed somehow darker and more mysterious than before. No, I wouldn't have it any other way. At the heart of the mystery lay the possibility of failure. Without that, without failure or even tragedy, neither the art nor the world would be so rich, so poignant.

At Last! A Rite of Passage

It was the coldest, darkest night of the year, and the chill night air was pouring into the dojo through windows opened wide behind me. I was sitting in one of the chairs provided for visitors, but on this holiday evening none of the usual crowd of onlookers was there and very few students—only the hardcore—were on the mat. Anybody with good sense would be home in a warm room with an open fire and holiday decorations and good food and drink, but I was up for my black-belt exam in just seven weeks. Sweat clouded my eyes and dropped off the end of my nose. Though my face was burning, my body was cold and clammy. I pulled my quilted *gi* jacket closer around me, but it was soaked through and felt as if it were turning to ice. Anyway, what difference did it make? What really concerned me—and though I was gasping for breath, I could examine the matter with a certain detachment—was whether I was going to die in the next two minutes.

I squirmed in my chair, panting for air. My heart felt as if it were beating out of my chest. The lights in the dojo seemed simultaneously too bright and too dim. Why wouldn't my heart slow down? Or was it speeding up? At this point, I remembered *centering*; that's what aikido is about, isn't it? If I was going to die, I might as well die centered. I put my attention on a point about an inch beneath my navel and rested my left hand over that point. There was no sudden deliverance, but somehow I felt better. My heartbeat slowed. My breath came easier. The lighting began to look normal again.

On this holiday night, as on nearly every night for the previous two months, I had been pushed to the limits of my skill and endurance. Five years earlier, when I first started aikido, I never dreamed I would be training for a black-belt exam, and now here I was, in the throes of a three-month-long period of intensive preparation, an ordeal by fire. The candidate for *shodan* (first-degree black belt) would be separated from the other students. While they were going through their regular training, he or she and an experienced *uke* would retire to the back mat and concentrate on the techniques that most likely would be required during the exam. Fifteen minutes or so before the end of class, the candidate would be summoned to the center mat. The other students would kneel around the edges and the teacher would call out various attacks. The evening would end with *randori*, which would continue until the candidate was driven beyond the limits of his or her stamina.

On this particular night, nothing had gone very well. At one point, I had said to myself, "I hope he doesn't call for *koshi-nage*," a hip throw I didn't feel prepared for. As if he had read my mind, Nadeau said, "Okay, George, let's see your *koshi*." And I had flubbed approximately every other one I tried. In the climactic *randori*, I did fine with the first two attackers but started tightening up when Nadeau called for a third. Then, God knows why, he called for a fourth, fifth, six, and seventh attacker in quick succession and I ended up flat on my back on the far edge of the mat, gasping for air beneath several bodies.

"You don't have to do this, you know," I told myself as I sat at the edge of the mat still trying to catch my breath. I considered the spectacle of a man my age working out so intensely with men and women, some of whom were young enough to be my children. Yes, it was quite mad. Even on that darkest of nights, however, I had no intention of quitting. A black belt would be a nice thing to have for my workshops, a sort of doctorate in movement. But it was more than that. It wasn't the belt or the credential or even the exam that brought me to the dojo night after night, but rather a more primitive longing. It was the ordeal itself that held me enthralled, the chance to confront difficulties and dangers within an ordered setting. At age fifty-two—at last!—a rite of passage.

Owning the Mat

I followed my teacher's classes faithfully through that chill pre-Christmas night, through the very last moment of the year. We were led in a special New Year's Eve training, from eleven P.M. to one A.M. When the horns blew and the bells rang, we simply continued our training, linking the old year with the new.

Three weeks before my exam, it was clear my techniques were solid. But something was lacking. One night, after I ran through an adequate but undistinguished *randori*, Nadeau had an idea.

"Your techniques are okay," he said. "The only problem is in your *air* It's the way you step on the mat. The key to your exam is going to be the way you get on the mat. The techniques will take care of themselves."

He mused for a moment, then stepped off the mat.

"Why don't you try this? When you step on the mat, say to yourself, 'This is *my* mat.' Be expansive, generous. Look around at the other people on the mat. Be glad they're here. Welcome them. Welcome them to your mat."

He showed me what he meant, then gestured for me to give it a try. I stepped on the mat several times, saying silently, "This is *my* mat." I liked the way it felt.

He continued. "Are you willing to take responsibility for this mat, to *own* it? That doesn't mean it isn't everybody else's mat, too. If you're big enough to own the mat as yours, you're big enough to let it be theirs, too."

Again and again I stepped on and off the mat, feeling better each time.

"You can even be a little cocky, George. That's not too bad in this situation. I think this will be your most important practice from now until your exam—not your techniques, but how you get on the mat."

The next night, when I was called to the mat, I wasn't there just "to take anything he could dish out," as had previously been the case, but rather to *own* the mat, to make it mine. This new *air*, and it alone, made a huge difference. I stepped on the mat expansively, looking around graciously at my attackers. When they came in, I welcomed them, moving swiftly to greet each one as he or she dashed toward me and throwing them easily to the mat.

My teacher nodded thoughtfully. No way was he going to say anything faintly resembling a compliment. For the next *randori*, he motioned to three of the more rough-and-tumble students along the edge of the mat. "Come in crazy," he said. "Unorthodox attacks."

The three of them rushed in with jerky, off-center grabs and strikes, something more like street attacks. But it was *my* mat, so I was pleased to welcome these eccentric attackers. The only difference was, they went down faster.

The next few nights were even better. My sessions at the center of the mat were transformed from ordeal to joy. I couldn't get enough *randori*. But my teacher wasn't going to give me a break. In the last few days before the exam, he chose to ignore me. Instead of calling me out, he let me sit on the edge of the mat and meditate.

A Beginner Again

The Sunday of my exam was a cold and rainy day, but the air inside Stanford University's Encina Gym was suffused with warmth and radiance. Aikido had grown dramatically since I'd first heard of it. Eight candidates were up for their exams and some one hundred fifty aikidoists from all over Northern California were coming in to witness the exams and participate in an aikido workshop led by a visiting sensei, a Japanese sixth-degree black belt I had never before heard of. Along the edges of the mat were hundreds of spectators, including what seemed to be almost everyone I knew—family, friends, friends of friends. The visiting sensei clapped his hands and led us in formal bows. It was my first glimpse of Mitsugi Saotome, who was eventually to play an important role in my aikido career. There was a chant, an introductory talk, and then the exams began.

I was the first on the mat, *my* mat. I had practiced the exam techniques over and over again, doing the best I could to create the exact exam conditions. Two weeks earlier I had driven down to the gym for a mock exam, which was filmed by a friend, the head of the Stanford karate club, so that I could study the film and make any needed corrections. The exam itself was almost an anticlimax, a ratification of what already existed. Later I realized that the process, the ordeal, was what really counted.

Ten minutes after the exams were finished, word was out that everyone had passed. The new black belts moved from one happy group to another, accepting congratulations. I noticed one of the chief instructors at our dojo, Bill Witt, standing to one side and grinning. He motioned me to come over.

"It's an old custom," he said, beginning to untie his own belt, "to pass your belt on to a worthy student. So if you'll just give me your brown belt to hold my jacket together   "

He handed me the belt—long, snaky, well used—and I handed him mine. With uncertain hands, I tied the belt around me. But there was no time to muse on my new status, which had once seemed as remote as Mars. The master class was about to begin.

Saotome Sensei had the compact body, good looks, and charisma that could have made him the star of martial arts movies. But what caught my attention and caused a shift, not just in my perceptions but in the center of my abdomen as well, was simply his *air*, the way he walked to the center of the mat to lead us in our ritual bows. It was his mat, no question about it. After the bows, he had several black belts with stout wooden staffs surround him. At a signal, they all rushed in to strike. There was some sort of motion—maybe a perturbation in time itself, I couldn't tell—and he was in a different place, easily throwing his attackers and taking their staffs from them. Then he was having two of our heftiest black belts grasp his wrists and pull his arms out to the sides.

"They're strong," he said in his pronounced Japanese accent, a mischievous smile on his face. "I can't get away." He struggled for a moment to show he was trapped. "But I can comb my hair." With a totally relaxed motion, he brought his hands up to mimic combing his hair and in that simple motion sent our hefty black belts flying head over heels.

"He's don Genero," I whispered to the aikidoist next to me, thinking of the most mischievous and magical *brujo* (Yaqui Indian sorcerer) in the Carlos Castaneda books then at the height of their popularity. Saotome had only recently arrived in America. I remembered hearing that he had studied for fifteen years with the founder of the art, had lived in his dojo, had trained with him almost every day. As he went on with his demonstration, I forgot all about my new black belt. I was totally fascinated, not just with this magical sensei's martial prowess but with his certain easy confidence and sophistication that I hadn't previously encountered in the aikido world.

I had never felt so much a beginner.

CHAPTER 7

Owning Your World

The idea of taking ownership of the training mat is too good to be restricted to a martial art. Ultimately, it can be applied to every aspect of your life. Start with competitive sports. Before entering the area in which the game will be played—the court, the field, the course—briefly center yourself. Be aware of the power that emanates from the *hara*, the physical center of your body. Feel your feet firmly connected to the earth. Start walking toward the field of play. How you walk will have a lot to do with how the game turns out. Move in a way that is both relaxed and powerful, both well controlled and open-hearted.

Now you come to an important threshold in this process. Say you're playing in a tournament at your tennis club and there's a gate that leads to the court. As you step through that gate, say to yourself, "This is my court." Pause for a moment after entering and let your eyes sweep over the entire area. As you do so, take ownership of everything involved in the game. Consider yourself not a mere actor in the drama that is about to unfold, but author, director, and producer as well. Take full responsibility for the court conditions, the wind, the light. Since you own this place, you can be a gracious host, welcoming everyone present—the spectators, the officials, the ball retrievers—with a friendly word, a smile, or a pleasant glance. This is all done in a relaxed, powerful, and centered manner.

Be especially welcoming to your opponent. He or she is your guest, someone who has come to help you play the game. The better the opponent, the better your game. If by some chance this opponent tries to intimidate you, don't intimidate back. There's no need to, for only the one who is willing to be intimidated can be intimidated, and you're in an entirely different position. Your opponent, no matter what his or her demeanor, is a welcome guest who is there to help you play a better game, and thus is always to be treated in a gracious manner.

Maintain this attitude throughout the warm-up and preparation period. Bear in mind that the game really began the moment you walked through the gate. And when the formal competition gets under way, give it your all. Express your high regard for your opponent by always hitting the ball in such a way that it is most difficult for him or her to handle. Never ease up. This is the finest gift you can offer a true competitor, for it allows him or her to play at the highest possible level. You expect the same in return. Still, you take the easy chances with the same centered, relaxed intensity that you devote to the most difficult shots.

This approach gives you the privilege of taking responsibility for the game you're playing, of fully *owning* it. Such ownership has its obligations, one of which is to play, as Elizabeth Barrett Browning said of the game of love, "to the depth and breadth and height/My soul can reach." And at the end, the measure of the experience has less to do with winning or losing than with the quality of the game.

But don't be surprised if you win.

The same guidelines apply in almost every situation you can imagine. You might try entering a restaurant as if it is yours, or a lecture hall, a tough business meeting, a courtroom. Some years ago, Betsy Carter, the executive editor of *Esquire*, was engaged in a civil suit against a New York taxi company. A taxi in which she was riding had had a serious accident in the Holland Tunnel and she had suffered injuries requiring extensive and painful reconstructive surgery. Now she was suing a company that had the toughest and most experienced personal-injury attorneys imaginable. I had described the above approach in a special issue of the magazine, and Betsy asked if I would give her a private coaching session as to how she might use it during the trial. We spent about a half hour in her office getting balanced and centered and visualizing the courtroom situation. She practiced saying, "This is my courtroom" and "This is my witness stand." We discussed how this would change her attitude toward the other people involved.

After the trial, the judge told Betsy that before she took the stand he was convinced the jury would find against her. After her testimony, he said, he had had no question but that she would win.

While performing at a higher level in sports and winning tough civil trials are important, the practice of owning your life has larger implications. Are you willing to own, to take sincere and positive responsibility for your relationships, your financial situation, your health, your spiritual life? To be reasonable, to avoid a foolish solipsism, we need to acknowledge that there are limits, things beyond our personal control. But perhaps there are fewer of these than we might think. And even then, being willing to own your life creates a context that is almost sure to enhance it.

CHAPTER 8

Adventure, Discovery, and a Dojo of Our Own

First impressions—oh, how they can mislead! One night back at the church, a new student appeared in the public class who somehow caught my attention. She was in her early twenties, slim, with large dark eyes and an abundance of dark hair. Her demeanor was humble and she spoke to no one, just kept her gaze focused intensely on our teacher. After class, someone told me she was living out of a car with her infant daughter. When I got home, I informed my wife that a homeless waif had joined our class.

Not exactly. Wendy Palmer, I later learned, was simply at a point in her life that tilted toward the hippie ethos. She had just left her husband and might have spent a night or two in her car, but she came from a privileged background— she was the daughter of a well-to-do Chicago family, the niece of Senator William Proxmire, a product of European finishing schools—and was destined to become a charismatic aikido teacher and workshop leader, a gifted writer, and an important person not only in my aikido career but also in the quest to bring aikido to a wider audience.

Night after night she showed up at the church and then at the San Francisco dojo that evolved from it, perhaps the most diligent student among us. As a brown belt, she was one of Nadeau's Four Fundamentalists. Her black-belt test came three months after mine, and I served as her *uke*. Now I was to experience the other half of the ordeal, attacking and being thrown by her countless times almost every night of the week as she prepared for the exam.

Sometimes, having done a certain technique so many times it was practically automatic, the two of us would carry on a casual conversation even during the attack and response—the ultimate in martial arts cool, but not a very good idea. We were engaged in such a conversation one evening when I rushed toward her and delivered a hard punch to the solar plexus. She stepped just off the line of attack, turned, and aimed a karate chop at my nose. My next step in this particular technique—I had done it many times—was either to block her blow or duck under it. In this case, however, I was so engrossed in what she was saying that I neglected to do either. The stars I saw when the edge of her hand met the bridge of my nose were pretty enough, but they didn't compare to the galaxy that exploded within my inner vision when the back of my head slammed down on the mat. Wendy leaned down over me and asked if I was all right. I was fine, I told her, as several varieties of liquid poured from my nose, mouth, and eyes. "Now I *know* you're going to have a great exam."

In aikido, we are taught to protect our attacker, and most of us do our best to follow that precept. But sometimes accidents happen, and so be it. This time it was entirely my fault. But even getting flattened as a result of too much cool seemed somehow amusing and delightful. Yes, aikido is dead serious. Aikido is also great good fun.

Beginner's Mind, Beginner's Foolishness

The workshops I gave during the period shortly before and after my first black-belt exam hold a special place in my memory. As the plane would take off from San Francisco, my heart would rise with it. I was buoyed by a certainty that the participants would gain something useful from the workshops, and there was always the possibility of something new emerging, some delicious surprise.

Whenever possible, I would take Wendy along to assist me. By then, almost every city had at least a small aikido community. A phone call was all it would take to have mats brought in, along with willing *ukes* so that we could entertain our workshop participants, and ourselves, with a demonstration of physical aikido. In Dallas, a fourth-degree black belt, a true sensei, brought students and mats and volunteered himself as our main *uke*. We had only recently received our first-degree belts. It didn't seem right for us to be throwing and pinning him. With a slightly amused smile, he insisted. He was considerate in his attacks and we got away with it.

"Beginner's mind" describes that condition idealized in

Zen in which the student is free of preconceptions and totally open and available for learning. Did we exemplify beginner's mind during that euphoric period? Beginner's foolishness would be more like it. In San Diego, before a large audience, we had no mats but there was a stage. Wendy stood directly behind me holding a knife by her side. At the moment she brought it up to thrust it at me, I spun around, took her wrist, and disarmed her. We repeated the demonstration several times, changing roles. There was no way we could have seen or heard the knife being raised behind us, and yet in this case we invariably moved at just the right moment. Members of the audience gasped.

How did we do it? I'm not sure. All I know is that at times of intense focus and strong intentionality, there seem to be agencies of perception and communication that haven't yet been measured by any instruments. In the years since these early adventures, as we'll see later, there have been rigorous experiments that tend to confirm the existence of such agencies.

This area of inquiry comes up naturally in aikido, an art in which considerable sensitivity is required to perceive the intentions of an attacker and therefore blend with, "become one with," his or her movements. In drawing life lessons from this art, I come back again and again to the question of undeveloped human capacities and the possibility that developing such capacities could increase our empathy with and understanding of others and perhaps mark the beginning of a new step in human evolution.

To even consider such a development requires a certain openness and a certain optimism. With its dedication to harmony, its mandate to protect the attacker, and its mission to make the world one family, aikido is perhaps the most open and optimistic of the martial arts.

Teaching Prison Guards

On another occasion during our adventures, Wendy and I drove down California's hot Central Valley to give a daylong workshop at the state's academy for prison guards. The training mats we had been promised turned out to be nothing more than disconnected pads that slid apart as soon as we started moving on them. What could we do? The prison-guard trainees sitting around the edges of the room were clearly less than impressed by a five foot five, 120-pound woman and a six foot four 175-pound man, both wearing white quilted jackets and long black pleated skirts. I figured about half of them as being hostile and the other half merely skeptical.

I looked down at the surface beneath me. I felt it with my bare feet. It was a single layer of hard industrial carpeting over concrete. "It's all right," I said. "Take the mats away." For the rest of the day, we did our demonstrations taking falls on what felt like granite. This foolhardy gesture gained enough respect among our hard-bitten trainees and instructors so that they would at least listen to what we had to say and try out some of our exercises.

After lunch, we were shown a collection of illegal weapons confiscated from inmates—ugly, jagged implements fashioned out of every kind of material you could think of. We were asked to show how we would take such weapons away from crazed inmates. Making no claims that our techniques would always be appropriate, we did a few take-aways using simple aikido techniques that we had practiced countless times, moving in and slightly off the line of attack, then grasping the wrist and turning it outward so as to throw the attacker down, pin him, and take the weapon away. It was all working out better than we might have hoped for.

The afternoon wore on. The room was hot, the ventilation poor. The instructors and trainees seemed exhausted. Then, without warning, the chief instructor—probably fed up with our talk of love and harmony and the possibility of using the minimum of force on prisoners—walked up to Wendy and grabbed her in a bear hug.

"How would you get out of this?" he said.

Wendy's eyes widened for a moment, but she didn't struggle. In our training we had learned that struggling, using muscular force, generally only makes things worse. Instead, she centered and relaxed totally while sliding and slithering downward, turning as she did so—and she was out and free. The instructor stood there for a moment, his face dark red. He started walking back toward his seat. Just as he passed Wendy, he wheeled and grabbed her from behind. Now he had her with her arms locked beside her and was squeezing with all his might, no question about it.

What happened next? All I can say is that Wendy began shrugging and turning her shoulders in a relaxed and curiously arrhythmic manner and once again was effortlessly free. This time the instructor stood there for a moment, then nodded his head thoughtfully and returned to his seat. From then on, the class was ours.

To this day, I don't know how we got away with the chances we took. Maybe it was just that the *kami*—the Japanese Shinto deities with a special affinity for the martial arts—were amused at our foolhardiness and were smiling down on us.

A Surprise—Everybody Can Do It

Early in my training with Robert Nadeau, he would perform feats that seemed to challenge my absolute faith in the materialistic scientific paradigm. Sometimes, for example, he would give us individual energy-balancing sessions. I remember sitting in a chair facing him; we both had our eyes closed and he held my hands in his. While he spent a couple of minutes tuning in, I tried to relax a knot of tension in my right shoulder blade.

"There's a tightness in your right shoulder blade," he said. "Send your awareness into that spot. Let it flow."

How could he possibly know that?

"There's excess energy in your head, especially in the eyes," he said a moment later. "You're like one of those balloon figures with all the air in the head. Let it flow downward."

I sat in silence, eyes closed, becoming aware of my head, which did indeed seem more alive than the rest of me. After five minutes or so, I felt a sort of tingling and aliveness rush down as far as my heart.

At which my teacher said, "Good. Now it's down as far as your heart."

The process continued, with me receiving feedback and encouragement until I glowed with a balanced sense of aliveness from head to toe. I had no idea how my teacher could tell exactly what was going on inside me. In fact, I would have been more comfortable if I could have denied the message of my senses. Nevertheless, the experience was quite undeniable, so I didn't deny it.

Around the time I got my black belt, it occurred to me that I might be able to do such exercises myself. I tried tuning in to the inner states of workshop participants and found it worked rather well. Then I had another thought: If I could do it, maybe they could, too. I began presenting it as an exercise for the entire group.

In this exercise, participants take partners and sit close, facing each other. Those who would be doing the tuning in (call them the "tuners") place their hands on their knees, palms up. Those who are going to be balanced (call them the "partners") rest their hands, palms down, on the tuners' hands. Both close their eyes and become as relaxed and centered as possible, paying particular attention to breathing.

The tuners are told to conceive of their own bodies as antennae, capable of accurately tuning in to their partners' bodies; in other words, feeling what their partners feel. Whenever they feel anything significant in their own bodies, they are to report it aloud, *as if it is in their partners' bodies*. For example, should a tuner feel tension in his or her abdomen, he or she might say, "Your abdomen is tense. Relax it. Let the energy flow from your abdomen to the rest of your body." Perhaps a minute or so later, the tuner feels his or her own abdomen relaxing and the energy flowing upward as a tingling feeling as far as the chest. "Good," the tuner says. "Your abdomen is more relaxed and the energy is flowing up to your chest. Now you might let it flow downward to your toes as well."

To my surprise, almost everyone in the workshop gained something from this exercise. Skeptics might say that the tuner's words would be positive and helpful no matter what was going on in the partner's body. True enough. It's also true that by comparing notes, the tuner and the partner generally discover that the tuner's perceptions of the partner's inner state is uncannily accurate—in location, intensity, and timing. In many cases, it's almost as if the tuner is perceiving exactly what's going on within his or her partner's body.

How can this be? Here I can't resist citing a well-known statement of the pioneering American psychologist, William James:

Our normal waking consciousness, rational consciousness as we call it, is but one special type of consciousness, whilst all about it, parted from it by the filmiest of screens, there lie potential forms of consciousness entirely different. We may go through life without suspecting their existence; but apply the requisite stimulus, and at a touch they are there in all their completeness, definite types of mentality which probably somewhere have their field of application and adaptation. No account of the universe in its totality can be final which leaves these other forms of consciousness quite disregarded.

More and more, as I continued experimenting in my workshops, I was discovering strong anecdotal evidence of alternative forms of perception, consciousness, and being that are perhaps innate in all of us, needing only permission for the first stages of their realization.

Our Own Dojo

When Wendy first began accompanying me to workshops, it was as my assistant. From the beginning, however, I noticed that during discussion sessions this once shy-seeming person wasn't really shy at all. When I encouraged her to join in the discussions, she was eloquent and precise. Years later, referring to that period, she told me, "I thought I was a hippie. You thought I was a teacher." She was a teacher.

While still a brown belt, in fact, Wendy started an adult-education aikido class at a high school in the San Francisco suburb where I lived. From the beginning, the class flourished. The high school was directly on my route to San Francisco. On some evenings, instead of driving a half hour longer to the San Francisco dojo, I would stop at the school and practice in Wendy's class, helping her out whenever she needed it. After a year, the class was canceled by the high school for administrative reasons.

So there she was, with some thirty committed students and no place to practice. What to do? How about start a dojo? She asked Richard Heckler and me to join her. Heckler was one of the Four Fundamentalists, a psychologist, a consummate athlete (winner of the hundred-meter sprint at the Pan American Games), and a talented aikidoist.

On the face of it, the idea was outrageous. Three brand-new *shodan* (first-degree black belts) would by no means be considered qualified to open a dojo under normal circumstances. But at that time there were very few black belts of *any* degree in the area. To establish the proper credentials for the enterprise, we invited our teacher to join us, to become a partner. He at first accepted, then demurred, probably figuring we didn't have a ghost of a chance of succeeding. Other higher-ranked aikidoists had attempted in vain to start a dojo in Marin County, in my opinion the most beautiful and desirable of the counties surrounding San Francisco, a place of redwood groves, unspoiled mountains, and sparkling water—and also a place where adequate space isn't just prohibitively expensive but generally unavailable.

Once again the guardian angels of the martial arts must have been smiling on us. We found a rental on the second floor of a building in downtown Mill Valley, a large, light, open space with exposed rafters and high windows, a space perfectly proportioned for martial arts—and a landlady who cared more about what was happening in her building than how much money she could get from its inhabitants. We have always been grateful to Betsy Broman and her son, Chris, who took over after her death with the same caring attitude.

Our village nestles up against an unusual mountain that rises 2,500 feet straight out of the Pacific. Mount Tamalpais is a habitat of deer and mountain lion and wild boar and many other wild creatures, and was once a sacred mountain for the Tamal Indians. The only artifacts found above 1,900 feet are religious in nature. I had spent many hours running and hiking its 175 miles of trails. There was no question about what we would name our school. Aikido of Tamalpais held its first class on October 22, 1976. Thirty-six students were on the mat that night. Since then, except for Sundays and "sitting down and eating holidays," Tam Dojo has held at least one class every day.

Over the years, several thousand people have stepped on our mat for a try at a lovely and maddeningly difficult art. Out of that imponderable number of seekers, we have graduated more than forty black belts, some of whom have gone on to start their own schools. We have become a way station for visiting master teachers from Japan and elsewhere who hold seminars attended by aikidoists from miles around. After Nadeau decided not to join us in partnership, he and the three of us gradually drifted apart, and we ultimately affiliated our dojo with the Aikido Schools of Ueshiba. Now our sensei is Mitsugi Saotome, the phenomenal martial artist I first encountered at my *shodan* exam, the most intellectual of the masters who apprenticed under the founder.

People have met at Tam Dojo, made longtime friends, become couples, gotten married, had children. Just to step in the door (many people have noted this) is to sense the palpable atmosphere that lingers in any place of powerful human interaction in a context of intense, long-term practice.

For me, Aikido of Tamalpais has also been a laboratory, an arena for experimentation and learning, not only in the martial art created by Morihei Ueshiba but in exercises and practices that can be offered to nonaikidoists, and even in certain realms that press gently but persistently against the boundaries drawn by mainstream Western thought.

CHAPTER 9

Context and Transformation

One dark night not long ago I awakened to the sound of music. But this was music of a power and immediacy I had never before experienced. Otherworldly harmonies from strings and horns rose toward a climax. An exotic percussion instrument, a sort of rattle, created an anticipatory vibration. An uncanny harp arpeggio swirled upward in the darkness.

I was in a corner room. The music was coming from both sides, from all around, more real than real. But what was such a huge orchestra doing in my neighborhood in the middle of the night? The air itself, the world all around me, was filled with sound, was made of music. My mind raced. What could it be? Maybe it was something unforeseen entering our world, a new phenomenon beyond my powers of comprehension.

After only a few seconds, there was a pause in the music,

then a voice in my ears. I reached up and in the darkness felt the earphones I was wearing. I realized that while listening to an audiotape of a book, I had been lulled to sleep by the narrator's voice. The music, descriptive of an eerie scene in the story, had awakened me from what must have been a deep state of unconsciousness. The volume of sound reaching my eardrums was equivalent to that which would have reached my eardrums had a very powerful orchestra been playing just outside my house. Awakening with no awareness that I was wearing earphones, I had had no place to locate the music except there. Was I "fooled"? Yes. Was the experience of eerie music outside my windows "real"? In a sense, yes. The sound of that mysterious midnight orchestra still resounds within me.

To put it another way: I awakened in the dark to the sound of an enormous orchestra. Then I heard a voice in my ears and reached up to touch my earphones. The music remained the same and my sense of hearing remained the same, but my *experience* was radically altered. There had been a change of context, and every change of context transforms experience. The word itself, derived from the Latin *con* (with or together) and *texere* (to weave), is descriptive. A context isn't just a passive container for our experience; it's an active process dealing with how we weave our experience together to give it meaning. Context is essential. It impels and directs our thoughts, emotions, and actions.

Effortless Power

Most of the exercises in this book involve a change of context. Take the two ways of rising from a chair under pressure described in Chapter 5. The physical motion involved is the same in both cases, only the context is changed. In the first case, you are struggling against a force that is holding you down; your shoulders and upper body are initiating the action. In the second case, you are by no means denying that someone is holding you down, but you are not struggling against that force. You are focusing your attention on your *hara*, and it is your *hara* that initiates the action and rises. Both in inner experience and external outcome, the second way can be radically different from the first.

One of the most compelling examples of context change to come out of aikido is what is known as the Unbendable Arm or, better, the Energy Arm. In teaching this exercise, I use the arm as a metaphor for rigidity in any aspect of life. Thus, a rigid arm can represent a rigid administrator, teacher, parent, thinker, and so on. After testing the resilience and power of rigidity, you have a chance for a radical change of context, the results of which you can also test for resilience and power.

Start by standing and extending one arm to a horizontal position. Either arm will do, but let's say it's the left arm this time. The hand should be open with the fingers spread and the thumb pointing upward. Have a friend stand to the left of your arm and bend it at the elbow by pressing up at your wrist and down at your elbow. Don't resist. Note that this exercise involves bending the arm at the elbow, not the shoulder.

Now that your friend has practiced bending your arm without any resistance on your part, you'll try two radically different ways of making your arm strong and resilient. After you've established each context, your friend will try to bend your arm at the elbow, adding force gradually. Bear in mind that this is not a contest but a comparison of two different ways of being powerful. The point is to see how much effort is required to keep the arm straight under pressure.

The first way. Hold your arm rigidly straight. Use your muscles to keep your arm from being bent. Have your friend gradually apply force to bend your arm. Resist your friend's force. Your arm might or might not bend. In either case, note how much effort you exerted in the process. Even more important, note how you feel about this experience.

The change of context. Take a balanced and centered stance and let your arm rise to the same horizontal position as before. This time, sense the aliveness of your arm and hand and the energy flowing from your shoulder to your fingertips. Now think of your center as the center of the universe and visualize or feel your arm as part of a powerful laser beam that starts an endless distance behind you, then extends through your arm and out past your fingertips, through any walls or other objects in front of you, across the horizon and to the ends of the universe. This beam is larger than your arm and your arm is a part of it. Your arm isn't rigid or tense. In fact, it is quite relaxed. But remember that being relaxed isn't being limp. Your arm is surging with life and energy. Assume that if anyone tried to bend your arm, the beam would become even more powerful and radiant, and your arm, as part of the beam, would be more powerful. Now have your friend gradually apply exactly the same amount of force as before in an attempt to bend your arm. Give little or no thought to the pressure on your arm. Just stay centered and relaxed and concentrate on being a part of a beam that extends to the farther reaches of the universe.

Note how much effort you expended. How do you feel about this experience? How was the second way different from the first? The overwhelming majority of people who have tried this exercise have found the second way, the Energy Arm, not only more pleasurable but significantly more powerful than the first, the Rigid Arm. Electromyographic measurements of the electrical activity in the muscles indicate that this subjective judgment is correct; the Energy Arm requires only about one-third as much muscular effort as does the Rigid Arm. It might give a little but is far less likely to collapse than is the Rigid Arm.

Why is this? For one thing, holding your arm rigidly involves co-contraction; that is, the biceps and the triceps are straining against each other. A muscle cell has only two possibilities: it is either firing or not firing. With co-contraction, many muscle cells in the arm are already firing and therefore not available for any other use. But the loss of power to co-contraction can't account for the tremendous increase of strength and resilience noted in the Energy Arm. Perhaps it is a manifestation of the subtle energy known as *ki* or *chi*, as we'll see in the next chapter. Whatever the underlying mechanism, it's the change of context that make this seemingly effortless power possible.

Here the implications for physical performance are obvious. And if we take the body as a metaphor for other aspects of our lives, the implications are even more significant. Imagine what it would be like if we realized we could be powerful without being rigid and resistant, not just physically but in other aspects of life as well. Note that in the attempt to stay rigid physically you were using a disproportionate portion of your energy in fighting *against* an external force. By so doing, you were *giving your power to the problem*, giving it away. In changing context, you focused on your own power by concentrating on your center and connecting it to the center of the universe, then extended it *beyond* the problem. By so doing, you took care of the problem much more easily than would otherwise have been the case, while remaining calm and centered.

The same thing holds for nonphysical problems. In workshop sessions with corporate executives, I have encountered organizations under attack from outside or beset by some serious internal problem that have focused so much of the executives' energy on the attack or the problem that they have lost sight of what made them successful in the first place, and thus have become ineffectual, swinging erratically between belligerence and panic. The remedy is clear: Don't deny the reality of the problem. Continue to deal with it. But do so from a calm, relaxed center that represents the true strength of the organization. Blend where it's advisable to do so. Extend from the organization's strong center *through* or *past* the attacker, toward the possibility of a positive outcome.

Whatever the situation, we change context through the interplay of language and bodily awareness, the words and music of the human condition. And when we do so—let me say it again—we transform experience and, in most cases, outcome. Context can limit and it can liberate. Changing it opens up new possibilities. It is ours to change.

CHAPTER 10

The Mysterious Power of Ki

One of the most ancient intuitions of our race is that there exists some sort of vital energy associated with life and intentionality, a subtle force that permeates and extends beyond the physical body. The intuition is robust enough to have survived the materialistic worldview, continuing to express itself in popular speech and science fiction. There are words for this vital energy in almost every language, many of them going back to the term for "breath"· *ki* in Japanese, *chi* in Chinese, *prana* in Sanskrit, *pneuma* in Greek, *mana* in Hawaiian, *wakan* in Sioux, *élan vital* in French, *bioenergy* in English, and "the Force" in *Star Wars*.

Whatever we call it (let's make it *ki*), this putative energy or force has sometimes been associated with special powers, especially in the martial arts, such as being able to break boards or stop attackers at a distance. But it's also thought of as the agency that produces vitality and health in living organisms or the entelechy that makes an oak tree out of an acorn. Some theorists have connected it to the evolutionary process. The French philosopher, Henri-Louis Bergson (1859–1941), calls the *élan vital* a current of consciousness that has entered matter, created living bodies, and determined their course of evolution.

Aikido, the "harmony-spirit-way," contains the word *ki* in its name and is especially mindful of its role. Rather than being special, *ki* is viewed as an essential element in every technique and, ideally, in every aspect of the aikidoist's life. "To train in aiki," the founder said, "one must drill in the development of *ki*. *Ki* is exceedingly complex, and we must risk our lives to master it." Though hard to put into words, *ki* is easily recognized. A throw performed with what we're calling *ki* looks different, feels different, and *is* different from one performed without it. To watch a practiced aikidoist easily, joyfully, even lovingly throwing three attackers again and again is to see *ki* in action. If you tried the Energy Arm exercise described in the preceding chapter, you might have a feeling for what is attributed to *ki*. Unlike the Rigid Arm, the Energy Arm has a relaxed and powerful quality to it, accompanied perhaps by the sensation of some sort of energy flowing through it.

But *ki* is more than an aid to technique. In the words of aikido master teacher Mitsugi Saotome: "It is the activity of life, the essence of spirit. *Ki* is vibration as light and sound are vibration. Sunlight is *ki*; thunder is *ki*; the wind is *ki*. It is tinier than an atom and more awesome than the galaxies. It is the vital essence of the universe, the creative energy of God. *Ki* fills the universe and all it contains from its beginning to eternity."

However we name it or conceive it, *ki* resists both definition and measurement. Yet it can be applied in seemingly effective ways. An ancient Eastern system of healing, for example, posits *meridians* (specific pathways in the body through which *ki* flows), *chakras* (major centers at which the energy is focused), and *tsubos* (points along the meridians at which finger or thumb pressure or the insertion of needles can correct energy imbalance in the body and thus aid healing). Though no one knows exactly how it works in scientific terms, acupuncture, which depends on this ancient energy system, has been approved by the American Medical Association as being effective in pain relief and the amelioration of certain medical conditions. And some major U.S. hospitals are experimenting with healers who pass their hands over and a few inches away from the patient's body, using what could be called *ki* in the healing process. In some hospitals, despite the skepticism and hostility of hardline critics, such practitioners are working with surgeons during major operations, with encouraging results.

The Energy Class

From the time my two partners and I opened Aikido of Tamalpais, each of us taught two classes a week. In addition to my aikido classes, I conducted an energy class that met twice a week. Within a few weeks, a group of some twenty students, some of them aikidoists, some not, had coalesced in the energy class. People came and went, but many of the original group stayed with the class for several years.

I led the participants in exercises I had already learned, then went on to create new exercises, group processes, and simulation games. We were willing to try almost anything. What didn't work we discarded. What did work we "put in the book." Sometimes I would ask the class members if they wanted to keep experimenting or to concentrate on the tried-and-true. The vote for experimentation was always unanimous. Some of the inventions of this period have moved out of the class into the world. For example, the Samurai Game™, a simulation game of extreme psychological intensity, has been presented to many thousands of people, mostly corporate executives, not just in the United States but also as far away as the Philippines, Indonesia, and China. In this game, participants become medieval Japanese samurai and in doing so give up all the rights and privileges of their present life and move across a line into a radically different realm of governance and consciousness from which they can view their own habitual life patterns with new eyes. There is a battle in which most "die," later to be "reborn." The game creates vivid memories. People who played it twenty years ago can still tell you exactly how they died.

Deeply engaged in this work, we found it hardly worthy of notice that some of the most successful and reliable exercises involved modes of sensing and communicating that haven't yet been measured by the instruments of present-day science, modes that might be summed up under the heading of *ki*. Many of the students learned to sense others from behind them or with eyes closed and in some cases even to describe their class partners' surroundings and experiences with some accuracy when they were on the other side of town. *And they tended to get better with practice.* Some of our experiences were clearly mysterious and wondrous, and yet, in the context of our class, they were commonplace and in the Zen sense "nothing special."

For example, an exercise I call the Synchronization Process aims at having participants locate their partners at a distance in a good-size indoor space filled with people who have been thoroughly randomized—and to do this with their eyes closed. I begin by leading the participants through a series of steps resulting in everyone's finding a partner to work with. Next I take them through inductions aimed at synchronizing their breathing and physical movement patterns with those of their partners. Several times during the inductions, I suggest that they think of themselves and their partners as merging their separate energy fields into a single field that is unique in the universe and greater than the sum of its parts. I offer them the possibility that, through their intentionality, they can be connected with their partners for the duration of the exercise by means of their merged energy field, no matter how far apart they might be.

The participants then leave their partners and walk around the room in a random fashion, eyes barely open. Finally, when the group is fully randomized and each participant disoriented by spinning in place with eyes tightly closed, all the participants raise both of their hands directly in front of them, palms forward, and rotate in place until they sense their partners' physical location. I then ask them to open their eyes and see if they have connected with their partners at a distance; that is to say, if the palms of their hands are directly aimed at their partners. This process—randomization, disorientation, and connection—is repeated three times.

First-time participants are usually quite startled by the number of direct hits. In one group of thirty-three people, only one person failed all three times. Fourteen participants located their partners with their eyes closed all three times, fourteen got direct hits two out of the three attempts, and four found their partners one out of three times.

The Synchronization Process isn't set up to be a scientific experiment. Still, its outcome and those of several other exercises that stretch or exceed conventional explanation have become so predictable and routine, with results seemingly so far beyond chance, that they have become axiomatic.

The Human Energy Field

How can we explain *ki*? Before we look for esoteric explanations, you might recognize that at every moment, day or night, your own body is generating and propagating electromagnetic energy, the ubiquitous energy that, depending on its frequency, expresses itself in the form of radio waves, heat, light, X rays, and so on across a broad spectrum. Every atom in your body is a submicroscopic electromagnetic device. Every chemical reaction involves an electromagnetic transaction. Your every thought, sensation, emotion, and intention is accompanied by electromagnetic activity in your brain. Every beat of your heart is triggered by electromagnetic impulses that cascade in swift and perfect rhythm the length of every artery and vein in your body. Your every muscular movement, even the smallest involuntary twitch, requires electromagnetic signaling and action.

And all of this can be recorded at the surface of your skin, and sometimes beyond; there are already instruments sensitive enough to measure your cardiovascular activity from several feet away. In addition, your body is surrounded by a cloud of ionized sweat that can be sensed at a distance by electrostatic indicators. And each of us projects an aura of radiant heat that can be seen in the dark thousands of feet away through infrared goggles.

Actually, the number of electromagnetic fields associated with the human body is beyond our power to calculate. Still, it's reasonable to suppose there must be a subsuming field for each individual that is everchanging yet unique—your own personal electromagnetic signature, as distinctive as your face, fingerprints, voiceprint, and DNA. Yes, there is a human energy field—negligible in terms of energy output, but extremely specific and highly organized in terms of information content. And information theory tells us that the more precise and coherent the information, the less energy is needed to carry it. The *Voyager* spacecraft, for example, could send radio messages all the way from Uranus and beyond to Earth using very little power because the frequency of its transmitters was so precisely in resonance with the receivers on Earth.

Rigorous experiments have recently shown that the effects of electromagnetic radiation on living systems depends not just on the intensity of the radiation but on its information; that is, its frequency and timing. Could it be that what we call *ki* is simply a complex and subtle type of information carried via electromagnetic radiation from one person to another? Such an explanation could help account for some of the effects attributed to *ki*—the healing power, for example, of a hand passed a few inches over a patient's body—but seems inadequate to explain effects at a significant distance.

The Zero-Point Energy

There are other possibilities. For several years, I've been getting letters, scientific papers, and popular articles on the subject of something called the zero-point energy from physicist Harold Puthoff of the Institute for Advanced Studies in Austin, Texas. On some of these communiqués, Puthoff has scrawled a tantalizing question: "Is this the basis for *ki*?" What he is referring to springs from one of the more bizarre predictions of modern quantum theory. According to this prediction, every cubic centimeter of space—and this includes the vacuum of outer space—contains untapped energy of enormous power. Physicists call it the zero-point energy, since it is the starting point from which all other energies are measured. The reason we don't experience this energy is that it exists in perfect equilibrium, pressing in all directions with equal force. But if somehow, through the power of our intentionality, we could influence the zero-point energy, even to the most minuscule degree, the effects would be significant, indeed.

Primitive shamans and Eastern sages have long assumed that we live and move in a vast sea of vital energy that supports and restores the material realm. The zero-point energy theory in its own way echoes that ancient spiritual belief. Physicist Puthoff proposes that the energy lost from atoms through radiation is constantly being replenished from the zero-point energy that pervades the entire universe.

Hyperspace and *Ki*

Still, a scientific theory that can fully explain *ki* waits to be born. Theorists on the frontiers of physics have various ideas on the subject. "*Ki* studies are purely empirical now," physicist Saul-Paul Sirag told me. "Any theory about *ki* will come from superstring physics." The physics that Sirag refers to proposes that all of the subatomic particles, the entire universe of matter, in fact, is composed of vibrating "strings" a trillion trillion times smaller than the atom. Matter itself is nothing more (or less) than the harmonies created by these strings. As with violin strings, the tiny superstrings can vibrate at an infinite number of frequencies, which helps account for the magnificent richness and variety of our material world. Those involved in this new field of study believe that superstring physics may eventually help us to unearth the Holy Grail of all the physical sciences: a single theory that unifies electromagnetism, the nuclear forces, and gravity.

What makes the theory difficult to shape is that the superstrings themselves exist only in hyperspace. Rather than having only four dimensions (one of time, three of space), the hyperspace of the strings has ten (one of time, nine of space) or maybe more. Understanding the complexities of this multidimensional realm requires a mathematics more powerful than any that currently exists. As the leading theorist in the field, Edward Witten of the Institute of Advanced Studies in Princeton, tells us, string theory is a piece of twenty-first-century physics that accidentally fell into the twentieth century.

Work on this fascinating theory continues apace. Recently, in fact, something called M theory has moved in with string theory. M stands for membranes, which are also called "branes," supersmall surfaces of from zero (a point) to nine dimensions that coexist with the superstrings. If this is difficult to understand, no problem; the physicists themselves are having trouble with it. The point is that these theories predict the existence of as-yet-unknown forms of energy. Could one of these energy forms turn out to be what we call *ki*?

Results Far Beyond Chance

All purely physicalist explanations of *ki* must remain speculative at this time, but evidence of its existence, both anecdotal and empirical, is not. And there do exist well-designed, rigorously conducted experiments that demonstrate presently inexplicable interactions between living systems at a distance. Between 1983 and 1996, for example, psychologist William Braud and anthropologist Marilyn Schlitz conducted thirty experiments in which "Influencers" attempted either to excite or quiet the electrical activity in the skin of subjects who were connected to a polygraph in a separate room. The tests, involving 105 influencers and 317 subjects, yielded positive results exceedingly far beyond chance ($p = .0000007$). Braud and Schlitz detailed and then successfully countered every objection that might be raised to the accuracy and integrity of these remarkable results.

No matter how well designed and rigorously conducted, physical measurements of subtle energies will probably always leave something out, since they are necessarily constrained by the present limitations of our instruments and the present boundaries of our senses. The history of science has shown that significant new discoveries tend not so much to provide final answers as to open new wonders, new worlds to explore. For now, let's simply assume that *ki* is subtle and pervasive, and that it in some way influences and is influenced by human intentionality. Even if this influence is minuscule, it could prove significant in the long run.

The Butterfly Effect

Chaos theory dramatizes the strong influence of extremely subtle events on highly complex systems citing the Butterfly Effect, the idea that a butterfly stirring the air in Tokyo today can transform a storm system in New York next month. Let's say that human intentionality expressed through *ki* is weaker by many orders of magnitude than are the ordinary verbal and physical means by which our intentionality has dramatically transformed the world. But *ki* is pervasive and over time might well create large effects in complex systems, including the human body, human society, and perhaps even the further evolution of our species.

Skepticism and Belief

Some martial artists claim the use of *ki* for far more powerful, indeed devastating, purposes. Maybe you've heard stories about the kung fu master whose open-hand strike is so fiery that it brands a handprint on the far wall. Or the qigong practitioner who can flip an attacker head over heels merely by gesturing from across the room. Despite personal experiences involving seemingly miraculous events, I've learned to exercise a certain skepticism when I hear such tales. But can I say without any doubt at all that they never happen? No. Life is too multifarious, too surprising for that.

After all our speculations, what remains is a deep respect for the strangeness and unpredictability of our existence in this marvelous universe. The years have taught all of us that scientific theories can change with the seasons. No matter how many studies we make or how advanced our math and physics become, final answers will continue to elude us. Seeking knowledge with an open mind, we embark on a journey during which the destination is two miles farther away for every mile we travel. And would we want it otherwise? How boring it would be, how conducive to despair, if everything were known, if there were no more mysteries. New discoveries open new possibilities for exploration. By its very nature, the world is unfathomable.

In a martial art that contains "the spirit of the universe" in its name, it is appropriate not only to seek knowledge without ceasing but also to stand in awe of the everlasting unknown.

CHAPTER 11

Taking the Hit as a Gift

Any unexpected misfortune, any sudden "hit," produces significant physiological and psychological effects. The cortex of the adrenal glands shoots a hormonal cocktail into your bloodstream; small blood vessels near your body's surface shut off, heart rate and blood pressure rise, your digestive process slows or stops, your muscles tend to tense up, your breathing becomes shallow. Your entire body might start. Your face could show alarm, grief, or terror, or perhaps turn pale as the blood drains from your head. You might be overcome by feelings of anxiety, annoyance, or anger.

These effects could be great or small, short-lived or long-lasting, depending upon the nature of the hit. In any case, they are generally energizing. Though unpleasant, they represent a gift of additional energy. The question is, how do you use such a gift? One of the most effective exercises that has come from aikido involves recontextualizing the energy of a hit as *ki*, then using the *ki*, not only to deal with the hit but to have extra *ki* left over to put to positive uses.

This approach is perhaps unique, but the phenomenon of misfortune being transformed into positive action is as old as time. The lives of historic figures are filled with stories of personal calamities that eventually have served to produce the greatness for which they are memorialized. As a young man, Franklin D. Roosevelt, for example, was characterized at best as a bright but rather superficial person and at worst a supercilious Groton-Harvard snob. The terrible attack of polio that struck him at age twenty-nine deprived him of the use of his legs but gave him a depth of understanding and an uncommon compassion for human suffering that helped to make him perhaps the greatest American president of the twentieth century.

But we don't have to cite such grand examples to bring to mind the unexpected blows that come to us in many varieties, from the merely bothersome to the truly tragic:

- Say you own an antique gold watch handed down from a grandparent, a watch you intend to bequeath to one of your grandchildren. Standing at the rail of a ship, you are showing it to a friend when it slips from your hand and drops into the sea.

- You and your spouse are driving along a lonely, winding road on your way to a country wedding, running a little late. Suddenly, there is a loud sound and your car wobbles to a stop. A tire has blown out.

- You've worked long and hard to complete an important report for your supervisor. You give her the finished product on Friday afternoon. On Monday morning, she walks into your office holding it. You smile inwardly, expecting praise. She plops it down on your desk. "I'm sorry," she says, "but this is very disorganized. We can't use it. It's not at all what we need."

- Your spouse comes home one day wearing a strange, pained expression. "I haven't had the nerve to tell you this before, but for the last six months I've been having an affair with your best friend."

There are, of course, many other hits that can come suddenly, without warning, some much worse than the above examples. Our most common responses to such unfortunate happenings tend to make things worse.

Immediate counterattack. Fighting back reflexively. "Whadya mean 'disorganized'? This is a damned good report!" Or you might start a terrible fight with your spouse, saying or doing things you would always regret. Such responses generally serve only to give additional power to the problem.

Whining. Being a victim. "Oh, no! Not *again*! Why do things like this always happen to me?" The victim's role is not only unattractive, it's self-defeating, inviting misfortune without redemption, forfeiting all chances of an eventual positive outcome.

Denial. "This doesn't bother me. I can handle it. I don't feel a thing." While it's tempting to steel yourself against the vicissitudes of life, to turn off or muffle your feelings, this path is a particularly dangerous one. If you practice turning off your feelings long enough, there's a good chance you'll get to be too good at it. You might become so insensitive that you honestly don't have the faintest idea, for instance, that you're seriously hurting your young daughter by ignoring or ridiculing one of her sincere concerns. You have to be aware of your own feelings to be aware of others' feelings. What's more, as numerous studies have shown, pent-up emotions can do consequential damage to your health.

We are generally offered very little instruction in dealing with these sudden hits, much less converting them into gifts that can change our lives for the better. "Buck up. Take it like a man." "Don't worry. Things will work out." "Stay calm. It's not as bad as you think." Maybe so and maybe not, but there are better ways. The procedure detailed below has been tried by thousands of people with remarkably good results. In fact, according to questionnaires given to people I've worked with, this exercise is invariably rated especially high at being of value in daily life situations. Many people have reported using the procedure within days or weeks of learning it. Sometimes it takes only minutes or even seconds to complete. In the case of truly terrible hits, however (the unexpected loss of a loved one, for example), it could take many long months to convert the hit into a gift. But the sequence I'm recommending remains the same.

1. *Experience and acknowledge what you're feeling.* This involves not only what you're feeling but also *where* in your body you're feeling it. Be as precise as possible. "When you said my report was disorganized and you couldn't use it, my heart jumped up into my throat. My mouth feels dry. My right shoulder is high and tense. I feel a slight nausea in my stomach and throat." This isn't to

suggest that you would say this aloud to your supervisor (unless he or she was also familiar with this way of expressing feelings). But make sure that you fully experience your own feelings or sensations and specifically describe their bodily locations, either aloud or silently.

Specifying the bodily locations of your feelings and sensations serves several essential purposes. First, it makes denial—the worst enemy of converting the negative to the positive—impossible. Second, it serves in many cases to mitigate or even eliminate the negative bodily tension or pain associated with the feeling. You can't very well release the tension in your abdomen, for example, without being aware that your abdomen is tense. Third, as shown in a controlled study inspired by this exercise, describing negative feelings in terms of bodily location is significantly more effective in increasing overall relaxation as well as alertness than is merely free-associating about those feelings. Finally, this practice prepares the way for the next step in the process.

2. *Center, ground, and breathe deeply.* Once you've fully experienced and acknowledged your feelings, bring your attention to your physical center. Also, if standing, bring your attention to the soles of your feet. If seated, bring your attention to your legs and buttocks on the seat of the chair, the small of your back against the back of the chair. Experience a deep and powerful connection with the earth. If inside a building, bear in mind that the building has foundations in the earth; you are connected to the earth. Breathe deeply several times.

3. *Become aware of the additional energy now available*

due to the sudden hit. Realize that the arousal caused by the hit is producing a prodigious infusion of energy. This energy isn't just physiological but rather mental, emotional, and spiritual as well. You've been shaken up, knocked momentarily off center, but in the very act of returning to center you've assembled this energy and brought it to a higher level—often a *much* higher level—than what existed before the hit.

4. *Use the energy of the hit wisely*. Begin thinking of all your newly assembled energy as *ki*, which, like money ("currency"), can be spent for any purpose you desire. It's up to you to decide how it's to be used. First, use it to deal with the immediate problem in as positive a way as possible. Then check to see if there's enough extra *ki* not only to deal with the hit itself but also to make other positive changes in your life. A personal story might show you just how this could happen.

My Worst Hit as a Writer

For writers, the saying goes, the best part of doing a book is signing the contract and getting the first check; after that, it's all struggle and sweat. A few months after signing the contract for one of my books, I sent in the first part of the manuscript, for which I expected to get the second portion of my advance. A couple of weeks later, on a trip to New York, I agreed to meet my new editor for lunch at one of those midtown bistros known for their literary clientele.

It seemed he could hardly wait for the obligatory glass of

sauvignon blanc before handing me an envelope containing a check for the first part of the manuscript.

"It's the most alive book I've read," he said, practically quivering with excitement. "It's sure to be a best-seller."

I floated out of the bistro. On the westbound flight, I felt the plane could make it all the way to San Francisco on my *ki* alone. Home again, I wrote with confidence and enthusiasm, finished the next portion of the book, and mailed it in. Two weeks passed, a month, two months—no response. Finally, I phoned my agent to find out what was up. Another week passed with no news. Then one Friday morning, just as I walked out the door to drive down to Esalen to give a weekend workshop, I heard the phone ring. Should I answer it or just keep going?

Something seemed to draw me back in. It was my agent. "Now we know why we haven't heard anything from your publisher," he said, his voice less alarmed than incredulous. He went on to tell me that there was not going to be any next installment of the advance. In fact, though the book was not even finished, the publisher was turning it down. Not only that, it was demanding that I immediately return all the money it had advanced me—which I had already spent. I walked out of the house in a state of shock, got in my car, and started driving south.

At first, I was too dazed to do anything except drive. By the time I reached the freeway, however, I realized I'd better start doing the exercise I was going to be teaching during the weekend workshop. My upbringing as a Southern male had explicitly and implicitly taught me to be brave, maintain control, never admit weakness, never display any sign of emotionality.

But how could I teach a new way of dealing with sudden and unexpected blows without doing it myself after this, my worst hit as a writer?

I started out by fully acknowledging that I had taken a terrific blow. I felt shocked, disparaged, deeply hurt. Where did I feel these things? Certainly there was a grievous pain in my heart, a hollow feeling in my solar plexus, a pressure in the back of my head.

Then there was the matter of money, the money I had already spent. How could I make it up? Maybe I could get another publisher, another advance. But what if I couldn't? What if the book—the book my editor had once called the most alive thing he had read—really wasn't any good? His earlier praise only made the hit worse, more devastating. I checked my feelings on this matter and discovered a root of fear in my abdomen sending tendrils up the sides of my chest.

Off and on for the next two and a half hours, I kept working with my feelings about the blow I had taken. At one point near the end of this period, I began to sense an insistent pressure just behind my eyes. I had told participants in my workshops that such a pressure was often caused by a need to cry. Then cry, I said to myself, and let the tears stream down my cheeks as I drove along at seventy-five miles per hour on I-280.

I passed Monterey and Carmel and came out on the Coast Road that led along high cliffs at the very edge of the Pacific, one of the most spectacular stretches of road in the world. It was about this time that I had acknowledged and experienced—over and over again—every possible feeling generated by the blow I had received. It was also about this time that one of the most marvelous, most euphoric infusions of *ki* I had ever felt began rising from my abdomen up to my shoulders, like the bubbles in a glass of champagne. The realization had come to me that I was gaining enough new *ki* from the hit not only to solve the book problem but also to have plenty left over for making some long-overdue changes in my life.

It was a period when I was stuck in a personal situation that was no longer working. Everyone else involved was ready, even eager, for the change; I was the one who was dragging his feet. Now, as the car seemed to guide itself along the sinuous curves and precipitous ups and downs of the Coast Road, the solution to the whole problem came to me all at once. When I arrived at Esalen, I went straight to the phone and started setting in motion the measures that I had so long delayed, which were to lead to a situation essentially right for me and everyone else concerned.

About the book: I ended up getting a larger advance from a new, better publisher. I successfully resisted paying back the first publisher. Upon publication, the book made the cover of three national magazines, including *Esquire*, and received major treatments in numerous and diverse U.S. magazines, including *Reader's Digest*, *Cosmopolitan*, *Christianity Today*, and *The Futurist*, plus more foreign magazines than I can now remember.

CHAPTER 12

Blending with Ki

When you combine the use of *ki* described in the "Taking the Hit as a Gift" exercise with the blending approach described in Chapter 3, the results can sometimes seem nothing less than miraculous. I was in New York a few years back on a promotional tour for a memoir of the sixties focusing on my adventures as a journalist during those tumultuous years. I arrived on a Sunday and had dinner that night with my daughter Mimi, son-in-law Jerry, and new granddaughter, Juliet, in their Manhattan apartment.

After dinner, my son-in-law asked what I would be doing that week. When I mentioned my Wednesday-afternoon date for an hour-long talk radio show hosted by Bob Grant, he practically jumped out of his chair.

"You've got to be kidding," he said. "There's no way I'd go on that show. His producers have asked me four times. *Noth-*

ing could get me on Bob Grant. You'd be out of your mind to do it."

I should mention that my son-in-law was Jerry Rubin, sixties revolutionary, one of the Chicago Seven, a founder of the Yippies, a man who when summoned to testify before the House Un-American Activities Committee went dressed as a Revolutionary War soldier, a man who was once quoted as saying his job was to make headlines.[1] The fact that even Jerry Rubin wouldn't appear on this show definitely got my attention.

"Why not?" I asked.

"Well, for starters, he's a fascist, sexist, racist pig." He followed that opening line with ten or fifteen minutes of general and specific horrors. "Now, have you got everything I've told you?"

I told him I'd definitely gotten it.

"Well, it's much worse than that."

The next morning I phoned Irene Williams, the public relations person at Houghton Mifflin who was handling my tour. "I'm a lover, not a fighter," I said. "I didn't realize—"

"It's all right," she assured me. "I can call and say you're not available."

She paused and in that brief moment of silence I realized I couldn't very well teach alternative methods of dealing with attacks and converting negative to positive energy without putting it to the test under difficult circumstances.

"It's all right, Irene," I said glumly. "No need to cancel."

---

[1]Tragically, Jerry Rubin was fatally injured in 1994 by an automobile while crossing a street in Los Angeles.

Irene and I met for a late lunch on Wednesday, then got to the studio fifteen minutes early. There was a loudspeaker in the lobby. As we sat there, we could hear Bob Grant disparaging and harassing his callers. He ended one call by screaming, "Get off my air, you damned liberal." The caller hadn't sounded very liberal to me. The incoming phone lines were obviously jammed. Grant was taking one call after another.

There was a commercial break and a small, slightly bent man carrying papers walked through the lobby, averting his eyes from us.

"That's Bob Grant," Irene whispered.

I felt my heart beating faster. The very presence of the man made me wonder if I was doing the right thing. Not long after that a producer appeared, introduced himself, and ushered me through a series of corridors to the studio.

"You'll notice," he said, "that we don't even have any left turns."

I couldn't resist rotating 270 degrees to the left at one turn to end up going to the right. The producer was not amused. He seated me in the studio and went back to the control room, which was separated from the studio by a large pane of glass. In the unnatural silence of the studio, I could hear my own heartbeat; by then, the rate must have been more than a hundred a minute. Had I done the wrong thing by coming on this show? I checked the feelings in my body, sat firmly in my seat, took deep breaths. I tried to think of the adrenaline rushing through my veins and arteries as *ki*, positive energy.

There was one thing I'd decided when Bob Grant walked

through the lobby. Whatever it took, I would get him to look into my eyes. I had heard that terrorists are trained never to look in their victims' eyes; otherwise they might humanize them. The studio, however, wasn't set up for easy eye contact. The counter between guest and host seemed unusually high, the wall of a fortress. My seat seemed lower than his. A large, old-fashioned microphone stood directly between his chair and mine.

Grant entered, his head turned away from me by at least forty-five degrees. As he approached his chair, I got up from mine leaned far over the counter—so far, in fact, that I was practically lying on it—and stretched my arm out full length, so that he could barely get into his chair without touching my hand. He recoiled from my outstretched arm as if it were a poisonous snake.

"Hi, Bob," I said.

Reluctantly, he gave me a limp handshake and for a moment, just a split second, our eyes met.

The commercials ended and Grant didn't waste a moment. "Well, we've got a good one for you here today!" he gloated. "His name is George Leonard, and he's written a book, *Walking on the Edge of the World*. And right here on the jacket—he probably wrote it—right on the jacket he says, 'Here's a unique and provocative memoir of that incredible decade we call the sixties, by a man who helped make it what it was.' Is that true, Mr. Leonard? Did you make the sixties—that ugly scar on our national history— did you make the sixties what it was?"

I took a deep breath, centered myself, and blended as best I could. "Well, there is something to what you're saying,

Bob." I went on to talk about *Look* magazine and its thirty-four million readers and about covering the civil rights movement and other protest movements in a sympathetic way. I ended by saying that although I certainly didn't create the sixties, nor did *Look*, there was definitely something to what he had said.

He went on to attack along another front, noting that I was associated with Esalen Institute—and isn't that nothing but a sex emporium? I told him that if I was sitting where he was and had formed my opinions from some of the things written in the press, I would feel just the way he did.

Having blended, I could go on and make my point. If you really came down to it, I said, there was probably more kinky sex going on in hotel rooms within two blocks of where we were sitting in midtown Manhattan during any one weekend than there was during a whole year at Esalen.

I was relieved that he didn't argue the point.

At the first commercial break, I leaned over the counter and said I'd been listening to his show in the lobby and that he certainly had a lively audience, the largest in the area, I'd heard. He said, well, yes, he had to be controversial to keep his ratings up. There seemed to be a slight note of apology in that statement. I asked about his previous experience and learned that he had had a show in Los Angeles. We began swapping the names of people we knew in common.

Grant's attacks continued after the commercial but his tone of voice was changing; there was less scorn and no screaming. And why were there no callers? Finally a call came from a young man in New Jersey. He had heard Esalen mentioned and wondered if I knew its president, Michael Murphy.

When I said I did, he asked if I had I read his book, *Golf in the Kingdom*? Yes, I said, not only had I read it, but Murphy had written part of it on my typewriter. The caller then asked if I knew where he could find Shivas Irons. Irons is the mythical but compellingly real Scottish golf pro in the book who offers enlightenment along with golf instruction. I dragged the conversation out for a while before telling the caller that I really didn't know where Shivas Irons was.

Neither Grant nor the producers (there were two men in the control room by now, both furiously shaking their fists at Grant) had the faintest idea what we were talking about. Under orders from his producers, I assumed, he proceeded to jump on me for my sympathetic treatment of the civil rights movement. "It's just because you're a Southerner and you've got so much guilt about what you've done to the Negroes."

I told him I had really looked at that and, in fact, had held a series of black-white marathons with Dr. Price Cobbs, a black psychiatrist, during which racially mixed groups talked candidly and heatedly about their deepest feelings on race for twenty-four hours without a break (meals were brought in), and one thing we'd discovered was that there were no whites entirely without prejudice and no blacks entirely without rage. So he had a good point, but it wasn't just about Southern whites.

Grant just grunted. Gradually, however, he was becoming less and less confrontational. We continued chatting during commercial breaks, and there were times, on the air as well as off, when we were beginning to talk as if we were old friends.

Another very strange thing was happening: There were no more phone calls, none at all, for the remainder of the show. I had a fantasy of Grant's million listeners sitting in stunned silence, wondering if they had tuned in to the wrong station or maybe that they had just entered the twilight zone. But why weren't they calling to attack *me*?

Near the end of the hour, Grant asked me what my favorite date in the sixties was. Without hesitation I named August 28, 1963, when Martin Luther King Jr. made his "I Have a Dream" speech in Washington.

"I'll tell you what my favorite was," he said. "It was July 20, 1969, when Neil Armstrong first stepped on the moon."

"Yes!" I said. "That would definitely be my second favorite—"

Which should have been enough to say, but I was sorely tempted to go a step further and do some mischief of my own. I had blended until my blender was bent and now I couldn't resist.

"Yes," I said, "I really love the space program." I went on to tell him I'd visited Mission Control in Houston and on another occasion had had lunch with astronaut Ed Mitchell, who had actually walked on the moon. I told him I was fascinated with everything about flight.

"You know," I continued, "I was a combat pilot in the South Pacific in World War II."

Over the years, I had discovered that men who see themselves as holding extreme rightist views tend to consider combat experience as the *sine qua non* of manhood itself, and are often quite discomforted when they meet someone who doesn't hold their views who has had what they feel they by all rights should have had. There was a nearly imperceptible slump to Grant's shoulders. Fortunately, however, he continued our increasingly genial conversation and perhaps became even friendlier. His last question blew all my circuits.

"Mr. Leonard, what is the meaning of life?"

Was this a joke, "the meaning of life"? Maybe, but I couldn't detect a hint of sarcasm. Rendered momentarily speechless, I started out by saying that, for me, we were here on this planet to learn and keep learning from birth to death. Warming to the subject, I went on and on about the human potential and how societies might use the maximum development of this potential in all citizens, regardless of ethnic background, creed, age, or sex, as a compass course for legislation and other actions.

I must confess I didn't stop there. The next day Irene Williams told me, "You were really playing your violin on that last answer."

There was little time left on the clock. Surely Bob Grant couldn't surprise me any more than he already had. But he did.

"I want to end this program," he said, "by reading the last two paragraphs of Mr. Leonard's book."

Those paragraphs were quite emotional and Bob Grant read them as I might have dreamed of their being read.

It was November and darkness was already descending over the city. As I wandered in the general direction of my hotel, I felt as if I were floating above the sidewalks of New York. But I wasn't fooling myself. I didn't for a moment think that Bob Grant was permanently transformed. By tomorrow his handlers would probably have forced him back into the shape that had gained their station a million listeners. (A few years later, in fact, Grant was fired for making a racial slur that finally even his employers couldn't abide.) And it wasn't just that my particular approach had produced a reconciliation where it might have seemed impossible, though that was nice. What lifted me a few inches off the sidewalk was that I had had the opportunity of looking inside an individual known for thriving on hatred and seeing, if only for a short while, the ineluctable presence of something akin to love.

That brief vision strengthened my faith in the words that Bob Grant had read with such genuine feeling: "that eventually the human potential will break through even the most powerful barriers that prevent the journey to destinations beyond our present imaginings" and that "unless we succeed in destroying ourselves, it will finally overcome any force that tries to stop it."

CHAPTER 13

Meditation in Action

How strange it is that such a simple act—sitting motionless, calming the mind, and letting the heart turn toward realms beyond the ordinary—can have such transforming effects. Yet the act of meditation, known to exist as far back in time as we can trace the human journey, can not only enhance the spiritual life but also significantly change bodily states for the better. More than two thousand studies published in reputable journals show that meditation can produce a great variety of desirable outcomes involving body, mind, heart, and soul. In their monograph, *The Physical and Psychological Effects of Meditation*, Michael Murphy and Steven Donovan present a review of such studies, which reveal that meditation can help to:

lower resting heart rate;

reduce both systolic and diastolic blood pressure (including systolic reductions of 22 mm HG or more);

produce significant changes in brainwave activity, among them increased frequency and amplitude of alpha waves (8–12 cycles a second), strong bursts of theta waves (4–8 cycles a second), and the synchronization of alpha waves between brain hemispheres, all of which indicate that meditators experience a state of alert relaxation and perhaps increased brain efficiency;

increase respiratory efficiency while the meditator is sitting and also while engaged in strenuous activity;

reduce muscle tension;

reduce blood lactate concentrations associated with anxiety and high blood pressure;

increase skin resistance, which indicates a lowering of anxiety and stress;

increase salivary translucence, while decreasing salivary proteins and bacteria, all of which helps prevent tooth decay;

reduce chronic pain;

heighten visual sensitivity, auditory acuity, and the discrimination of musical tones;

improve reaction time and responsive motor skills;

improve concentration;

help relieve addictions;

improve memory and general intelligence;

increase energy and healthy excitement; and

increase dream recall.

At many dojos throughout the world, you'll find meditation offered as a part of or an adjunct to physical aikido. The founder of the art was deeply involved in practices aligned with meditation. All his life, and especially in his later years, he spent many hours in meditative sitting, bowing, praying, and chanting. On some occasions, he would stand and whirl his *jo* (wooden staff) above his head, creating a vortex connecting heaven and earth, at the same time emitting an eerie, high-pitched sound.

I've asked many people who've trained with O Sensei to reproduce this sound, but all of them have begged off, telling me they couldn't even come close. What we do know is that O Sensei was a devotee of *kotodama*, the Shinto science of "sound-spirit." According to *kotodama*, the universe was born as an incredibly dense, energetic point represented by the vibration *su*. This vibration, just as in the big bang theory of modern physics, was conceptualized as expanding outward in terms of various other vibrations, each represented by a different sound, to create the universe as we know it.

Could this intense and highly active chanting practice be called meditation? According to an old Taoist saying,

Meditation in action is
A hundred times
No, a thousand times
No, a million times greater
Than meditation in stillness.

Discounting the numerical hyperbole, there's much truth here. We might say, in fact, that sitting meditation ultimately aims at the maintenance of the meditative state during all of life. Zen practice includes not just sitting meditation but also *kinhin*, a slow meditative form of walking, and urges its practitioners to maintain the meditative state while eating and doing their "temple work." The same is true of other meditative practices.

My aikido classes begin with a short meditation followed by a ritualized series of movement, breathing and stretching exercises. After practicing a certain technique a number of times, I'll sometimes have the students return to their places along the edge of the mat and meditate for several minutes, then repeat the same technique as if it were part of their meditation. The difference between the technique done before the meditation and the same technique done after the meditation is easily apparent; the students' movements seem more natural, more flowing, less forced.

The meditative state is even more important in *jiyu-waza* (freestyle) and *randori* (multiple attack). In these advanced practices, it's important to be relaxed, grounded, centered, balanced, and energized, and to remain poised, without expectation or prejudgment, in the present moment. Linear, rational thought ("Since the attacker is aiming a punch at my chin, I'll step in and aside, blend, and bring his arm down and around in a *kaiten-nage* throw") would be disastrous. One of the benefits of meditation listed above is an improvement in reaction time and responsive motor skills, made possible in part by the very *presentness* of the meditative state, a condition in which thought and action become one. I have enjoyed rare moments in *jiyu-waza* or *randori* during which, set free from the prison of words, I find myself in a place of utter clarity and calm, where it is always *here*, it is always *now*, and there is only harmony, harmony. After such an experience, I can't help but think of two lines from the ancient Chinese philosopher and poet, Lao-tzu:

> The Way lies in not doing
> Yet nothing is left undone.

To practice aikido in a meditative state can bring great joy. But it's no less wonderful to watch twenty or thirty students doing *jiyu-waza* and see the smooth, softly undulating waves created by a short session of meditation spreading in concentric circles over a sea of motion on our training mat.

Easy Instructions, Endless Possibilities

Getting started in meditation is surprisingly simple. Wear clothing that doesn't constrict the body. Make sure your belt isn't too tight. Assume a sitting position on a floor cushion with your back straight and your legs crossed or sit in a straight-backed chair. Place your hands on your knees, either palms up or palms down. Or they can be cupped in your lap with your thumbs touching, as they are in most Zen practices. Experiment, then stick with one method; your particular way of sitting can become like a home to you, a familiar and comforting place.

An erect sitting posture, either on a cushion that elevates your seat from the floor or in a chair, will help you stay alert during the meditation exercise. If, during the exercise, you find yourself slumping, gently straighten your spine and rebalance yourself. Relax your shoulders. An alert yet relaxed posture tends to produce an alertly poised state of mind.

In some forms of meditation, the eyes are kept closed. It's also possible to meditate with eyes open, which may help you stay awake and keep your mind from drifting. Maintain a soft and relaxed focus, looking downward as if you were gazing at a gentle stream.

Once your posture is comfortable, let your belly expand with each breath. Make sure your breath isn't confined to your chest. Anchor your attention on the rise and fall of your breathing. Focus on your lower abdomen and return to it whenever your mind wanders.

Don't try to stop thinking—a daunting task. Instead, remain calmly present to your stream of consciousness; witness each wayward thought, then let it pass. Some meditators repeat a mantra, a word or phrase or sound, to help focus attention and stop the verbal chatter of the mind. Others count their breaths. You can experiment with these different methods, but once you've settled on one that works for you—whether it's focusing on your breath, a mantra, or your stream of consciousness—stick with it. Moving from one technique to another can distract you from the deeper rewards of meditation.

You might start with short periods of meditation, five or ten minutes, then, if you wish, lengthen them. As you continue meditating, you may realize that you are more than any idea or mental picture, more than any emotion, more than any impulse, more than any bodily process, more than any pattern of experience with which you typically identify. You may find that this *something more* expresses itself in religious terms, or simply as a boundless space or unbroken essence that connects you with everything.

In any case, the meditative experience of awareness beyond the ordinary sense of self can produce a buoyancy and calm that spills over into the rest of your life. Something as humble as washing the dishes in a meditative state can bring the same buoyancy and calm. Rather than feeling yourself rushed, anxious to get the job over with, settle into the task of dish washing as if it were a meditation. Check your posture. Relax your entire body. Let your belly expand with each breath. Do not hurry. Be aware of and appreciate your every motion. Stay in the present moment. At the end of the task, you might be surprised to find that, by not hurrying, you finished considerably sooner than would otherwise have been the case.

There are indeed many activities that easily lend themselves to meditation in action: walking, dressing, bathing, doing any repetitive task. And finally, every aspect of living might well benefit from one of the simplest and most profound practices known on this planet.

CHAPTER 14

Zanshin: *Continuing Awareness*

A few years ago one of my LET students (not an aikidoist) told me she had discovered a real master of Chinese fighting sticks and would like to schedule a public demonstration at our dojo. I was reluctant. Movement space was extremely rare in Marin County and we were generally fully booked. Anyway, what did she mean by "real master"? *Master* is a word I rarely use; better to say that one is on the path of mastery. But my student was persistent and I finally relented.

A small audience paid a nominal fee to witness the event, which occurred on a Saturday afternoon. The putative master was wearing a gym suit rather than martial arts garb and seemed a bit surprised when I asked him to remove his gym shoes before getting on the mat. His technique was impressive. The sticks whirled and created interweaving patterns as they whistled through the air. At the end of each technique, however, he simply went limp, walking carelessly around the mat as he lectured on his art. These shifts continued throughout the event. While actually working with the sticks, the "master" carried himself well and moved gracefully; at the end of each technique, his shoulders slumped, his movements became sloppy and careless. At one point, he dropped a stick and seemed to have trouble picking it up.

While I appreciated this man's technique, I would be hard-pressed to call him a master—perhaps he was not even on the path of mastery. There was one fundamental problem: He was sadly lacking in *zanshin*.

Zanshin, "continuing awareness," is, in the words of my teacher, Mitsugi Saotome Sensei, "the extension of the spirit, the continuation of energy and awareness that prepares for the next action   In the study of aikido, taking *ukemi* [playing the part of the attacker] or executing techniques is not the end of the process; it is the beginning of the next action.   You must remain constantly alert, aware of your partner in practice, aware of all the movement around you, ready for the unexpected in any direction.   *Zanshin* is the future, but *zanshin* is also now. The quality of your *zanshin* is the quality of your aikido." The quality of your *zanshin* is also the quality of your life.

In my classes, *zanshin* plays a key role. Sometimes I tell my students that for the next half hour I won't be watching their techniques; I'll only be watching what they do, how they act, how they comport themselves *between* techniques. What happens? By becoming alert and aware between techniques—that is to say, *all the time*—the students invariably improve their techniques.

On other occasions, I break the class into groups of three so that each of the three can take turns being attacked by the other two. After ten minutes or so, I get everyone to close his or her eyes, then I ask various students to name—with eyes still closed—the aikidoists in the threesome practicing nearest to them. The first time I tried this exercise, hardly anyone could name all three, but it didn't take long for students to expand their awareness to include not just those in their own group but those all around them.

The purpose of this exercise is to develop what I call "full mat awareness" and to prevent tunnel vision. While it's all to the good to concentrate on your training partner, it's just as important, as Saotome Sensei has said, to be "aware of all the movement around you, ready for the unexpected in any direction." Tunnel vision is particularly dangerous in flying combat missions. In a phenomenon known as target fixation, pilots have been known to become so fixated on their target that they fly their plane straight into it. Combat flying requires a high degree of *zanshin*, the ability to register details while remaining aware of the larger picture, to focus on the target while staying alert to the possibility of enemy attacks, to consider the future while staying in the now.

You don't have to take up a martial art or go into combat to recognize the need for *zanshin*. Daily life provides challenge enough. Changing several lanes to get to an exit ramp on a freeway packed with speeding cars demands as much physical/mental/sensory coordination as flying low-level strikes. In fact, informal experiments with NASA in the 1960s showed it takes more brain activity to drive on a busy Los Angeles freeway than to pilot a lunar landing simulator. Aside from such heroic activities as combat flying and freeway driving, it's valuable simply to cultivate a sense of *presence* at all times, to increase your everyday awareness, to become, as novelist Henry James would have it, a person upon whom nothing is lost.

A More Vivid Peace

But isn't it nerve-racking to stay constantly alert and aware? Not necessarily. In the 1980s, my wife, Annie, and I led certification programs for Leonard Energy Trainers. We were determined to make these programs as rigorous and memorable as possible. They were held at Esalen Institute, which is perched on a 120-acre plot of land squeezed between mountains of the Coast Range and the Pacific Ocean along nearly a mile of the Big Sur coast. There were broad lawns leading to the edges of cliffs, which dropped straight down to the sea. There was a lovely organic garden and a small farm, and also areas of forest and brush and a primal redwood canyon. For eight weeks, in this spectacular setting, the candidates for certification were put through rigorous sixteen-hour days, from six in the morning until ten at night, six days a week. They were expected not only to learn how to present LET exercises, but also to meditate, practice aikido and *bokken* (wooden sword), do aerobic exercise for an hour a day, participate in warrior games, and, through it all, to maintain *zanshin*.

One of our candidates was a recently retired Marine lieutenant colonel named Jack Cirie, who had completed two tours of duty in Vietnam and had received a chest full of medals for heroism. He saw no limits as to how far he could have gone had he stayed in the Marine Corps. He was a consummate athlete: a most valuable player in football at Yale, a regimental boxer in the Marines. He was a fine musician, singing folk and ethnic songs with his guitar in a rich baritone. He loved poetry and philosophy and was the kind of leader we all dream of—firm and decisive but not inflexible, invariably high-spirited. His slightly conspiratorial grin promised he was about to let you in on something wonderful, and he often did. More than anything, he brought with him a sense of the zest and tang of life.

With all this, Jack had chosen to leave the Marines, to become a warrior for peace. Both he and I had witnessed the horrors of war. At the same time, we had experienced its enduring appeals. For many people, their wartime experience had been the most vivid and memorable chapter in an otherwise dull and tedious book of life. Before we met, each of us had come to the conclusion that to achieve a lasting peace, it's important to oppose war, but that it's also important to create a more vivid peace.

After doing our program twice in two years, Annie and I were exhilarated but exhausted. Jack had been certified in our second program and had gone on, as a civilian, to lead an experimental six-month training for U.S. Army Special Forces troops at Ft. Devin, Massachusetts, a program that included meditation, aikido, and biofeedback along with the Green Berets' regular training. When that was completed, Annie and I asked him to lead our third program at Esalen.

We agreed to join him during the first, middle, and last of the eight weeks. It was during the final week of the training Jack led that the need for *zanshin* had reached its highest point.

The idea came from the Samurai Game™, which Jack had played and then co-led with Annie and me. In this game, some of the make-believe samurai are armed with *shuriken*, the deadly throwing stars that are used by the ninjas you see in the movies. But instead of tempered steel with razor-sharp points, our *shuriken* were the metal tops of frozen orange-juice containers, which we would throw underhanded like tiny Frisbees. These faux *shuriken* make a highly satisfying *pwoingg* sound when they hit someone, then clatter metallically when they fall to the ground. Thrown skillfully, they fly straight for about fifteen feet, then tend to swerve off course; you have to get close to your target to maximize the possibility of a hit.

Using these weapons, Jack developed an ambush game that we played throughout the entire last week of the training. Candidates and leaders were equal participants. Interior spaces were off limits, but an ambush was possible at any moment out-of-doors. Each of us carried two or more *shuriken* for ambushing others in our group. This meant that just going from our cabins to the lodge for a meal was an adventure. Every tree, every bush, every structure might hide an ambusher. As the week went on, the game became more and more intense, the need for *zanshin* more and more imperative. Some candidates climbed trees, eased their way out on branches that overhung paths. Others lurked on the roofs of buildings. One candidate scrunched down in an open-top wooden structure that held compost. You never knew when a *shuriken* would come sailing your way. We didn't keep score; it was simply a matter of honor to ambush as many members of our training group as we could while not being ambushed ourselves.

A rushing mountain stream bisected the property; there was a narrow wooden bridge over it that could have graced any Japanese samurai movie. To get to the round meditation house at the edge of the stream, it was necessary to walk down a steep hill past the bridge, then turn and take a path that led under it. A half hour before meditation one dark morning (it was November), Jack secured the jungle hammock he had used in Vietnam to the far side of the bridge, away from the direction the candidates would come, then lay in the hammock. As he heard each of them approach, he threw his voice—a skill he had learned in combat—to make it sound as if he was already in the meditation house. As each candidate passed beneath him, he reached down and gently touched him or her with the tip of his *bokken*. Not one looked up until touched. Not one escaped.

To get revenge, a candidate named David Dimmick climbed stealthily to the roof of Jack's cabin in the darkness a half hour before meditation time. He stretched himself out on the arbor that Jack would have to pass under when he came out of his cabin. He lay there in absolute stillness, ready to touch Jack's shoulder with his *bokken*.

Jack dressed and started to go out the door. When his hand touched the doorknob, he had an uncanny feeling that something was amiss. He turned and went to the balcony at the other end of his cabin. The balcony stood at the edge of a cliff about a hundred feet above the ocean. Jack climbed over the railing, worked his way along the cliff, cleared the building, and continued down to the meditation house on the other side of the property. David was considerably late for meditation.

A World Come Alive

More and more, as that magical week drew near an end, Jack and I focused our efforts on each other. Neither of us had been hit. The contest between us was delicious, each of us stalking, each of us escaping, not only each other but the other members of our group.

Of many vivid moments, one glows in my memory. It was early in the morning. All of Esalen except our group was fast asleep. As I started walking toward the meditation house, a strangely radiant object came into view behind the cypress trees, a smoldering globe of copper-red hanging low above the sea. For a moment I was disoriented. How could this dusky sun be setting at five-thirty A.M.? I had to convince myself that it was not the sun at all but only an enigmatic moon preparing to extinguish itself in the dark Pacific.

And here came Jack, that jaunty walk more a minstrel's than a soldier's. I ducked behind the first cabin in a row of cabins. He passed without seeing me. I followed him onto the long wooden walkway that fronted the row. He was walking fast. The walkway was protected; Jack thought he was safe. But I was behind him, my every step striking the walkway at the same instant as his so that the sound of my feet would be swallowed up in the sound of his. But I was taking longer steps, my *shuriken* held in my right hand, ready to throw. Near the end of the walkway, Jack suddenly stopped and turned. But it was too late. My *shuriken* was already sailing toward him, in slow motion now, seemingly sustained in flight not by momentum or aerodynamics but by the magic of the human mind, to gently find its mark in the center of his chest.

The ambush game continued and there was no winning or losing. There was only the rare gift of total awareness in every moment. You might think that the constant expenditure of such mental and sensory energy would prove exhausting or even nerve-racking. And, yes, it's true that all of us need to kick back at times, to relax completely, putting aside all agendas, all immediate responsibilities. But actually my experience was just the opposite of what you might think.

During that week of intense *zanshin*, I became calmer and calmer. And a wondrous thing began to happen. All the objects of my experience—the bridge, the compost enclosure, the propane tank, every bush, every tree, everything within the radius of my awareness that could have served to conceal an ambusher—began to take on incredible significance and life. They were like the objects in a stage set that start out in total darkness and then are slowly illuminated, one after another. It was as if I had never really seen them before. Now everything in my visible world was vibrantly alive and I was a part of it all.

You might say that this was just a game, and a child's game at that, and that if the *shuriken* had been real I wouldn't have felt that way. I would certainly not have wanted to play the game with real *shuriken*. Still, I must say that during the twenty-eight-day period when I flew twenty-one low-level strafing missions in the Philippines, some lasting upward of five hours, I slept like a baby. Though two of my eighteen squadron mates were killed during that period, the missions were not heroic. Still, there was something deeply satisfying in simply being so fully engaged. The wood-framed canvas army cot I slept on was two inches shorter than my body, I used my flight jacket as a pillow with the top of my head hanging over the frame of the cot. But never have my dreams been so sweet.

This isn't by any means meant to glorify armed conflict. There's very little or nothing that can justify the destruction and suffering of even one day of all-out war. Nor am I saying we should necessarily play warrior games. I'm just raising the possibility that the *absence* of engagement, the hours spent in one or another form of channel-surfing, is actually the chief cause of our anxiety and mental exhaustion, the sleep of the spirit the chief cause of our despair. It's an ancient message that comes down to us from every great wisdom tradition: We are asleep. To know God, to live a good life, we must wake up.

To do so, we don't need war or warrior games or anything special. Just look into the eyes of and truly *see* a loved one or any young child, and juxtapose this *seeing* against the brevity of life and the eternity that stretches before and after it. Just take a walk and open your inner eyes to the *aliveness* of everything around you. Every moment of existence, if only we could see it true and clear, is incredibly vivid, even on a drowsy summer afternoon. *Zanshin* isn't merely a condition of preparedness for martial artists. It's a wake-up call to life for all of us.

A Warrior's Death

A little over three years after we played the ambush games, Jack Cirie died. It was sudden and unexpected; he spent only one day in bed at home and a few hours in the hospital. What happened, as best could be surmised, was a total, catastrophic breakdown of his entire vascular system, probably the result of exposure to Agent Orange in Vietnam.

Our friendship had continued to deepen up to the time of his death. He supervised the production of the Samurai Game™ for some thousands of managers and executives. He visited us in Marin County. We went to his wedding on Orcas Island, then, a few months later, to his memorial service in Seattle. Annie and I still can't quite believe he's dead— and the same is true for his other friends. Sometimes, when the doorbell rings, we expect to find him there, that tantalizing grin on his face, bringing with him some new toy, some new game to play, some spellbinding story to tell.

Jack always ended the message on his answering machine with two words: "Stay alert." For a while, I tried to do the same, but it never quite came off. There was no way I could capture his unique inner pulse, his way of joining presence and power with a sense of fun. Now when I think of *zanshin*, I hear Jack's message: two words containing the richness of existence, the sheer joy of living.

Stay alert.

CHAPTER 15

Aikido Walking

New students often ask me how they can practice aikido at home alone. I have to tell them that the lack of a partner does limit what you can practice. Aikido involves a radical way of dealing with incoming energy. To learn its techniques, you'll need someone to work with so that the two of you can take turns being the *uke*—that is, being the incoming energy, the attacker. There are, of course, certain moves you can practice alone, but aikido has none of the elaborate *kata* (solo practice forms) so familiar in the striking and kicking arts.

There is, however, one accessible and effective way to develop many of the basic qualities required in aikido and also gain a number of its benefits, and that is simply through walking. This seemingly commonplace act is actually a great wonder: stately, graceful, and efficient, an essential mark of being human. The journey of our lineage toward the large brain, culture, and consciousness took an essential and irreversible turn with the evolutionary gamble of the upright stance and unique bipedal walking of our hominid ancestors. We are so accustomed to it that we are unaware of how marvelous walking is—this supple, undulating movement, this easy, liquid flow of movement unlike that of any other creature.

For one thing, walking offers us the safest and most convenient means of staying fit. Numerous studies in recent years have shown that as little as four brisk half-hour walks a week can make the difference between well-being and the sedentary lifestyle that brings as many health risks as smoking a pack of cigarettes a day. But walking is much more than a means of locomotion and an agency of fitness. It expresses not only the uniqueness of our species but also the singularity of each of us within this species. With each step you take, you are inscribing your signature in motion. To know how a person will dance, play sports, make love, converse, write, or even think, look very closely at how he or she walks.

For example, people who work with a forward lean, as noted in Chapter 5, are likely to get ahead of themselves in everything they do. Those who walk rigidly are likely to be rigid thinkers. Angry people almost always reveal themselves by how they walk, imparting unnecessary force on the ground with every step. Depressed or gloomy individuals express their mood through the slouch of the shoulders, the collapse of the pelvis. Fearful people walk with shoulders high. We have seen (also in Chapter 5) how muggers pick their victims not primarily by how large or strong they seem, but simply by how they walk. When a martial arts teacher strides to the center of the mat or a speaker to the podium, those watching are given immediate and significant information about that person and are making immediate and significant judgments, whether conscious of it or not.

Clearly, then, changing the way you walk can have profound consequences. It can't be done overnight; we become what we practice and we have been practicing walking since infancy. Any significant change will probably seem strangely exaggerated; if you've been walking with your shoulders slumped, simply bringing them to normal may make you feel self-conscious or queasy. It might take weeks or months before your new posture feels natural to you. And by the time it does, you'll probably have made significant changes in the habitual mental and emotional attitude expressed in the slumping of your shoulders. But you can start the change process now—a commonplace adventure that leads to extraordinary results. Bear in mind that you've already been introduced to concepts and practices that contribute to excellent walking: centering, meditation in action, *zanshin*. Now let's get right down to the act itself. Let's do some aikido; that is to say, let's take a walk.

First Steps

You need no special equipment except a pair of good walking shoes, and in some circumstances—indoors, on a grassy surface, at the beach—you need no shoes at all. Take a few moments for balancing and centering before starting.

While it's not necessary to go through this entire procedure every time you do aikido walking, you may find it useful in getting off to a good start.

Stand with feet shoulder-width apart. Breathe deeply. Let the breath expand your abdomen, not just to the front but also to the back, the sides of the pelvis, the floor of the pelvis. Imagine a beam of *ki* from the center of the earth moving straight up through your body, out of the top of your head, and upward to the zenith of the heavens. Then imagine that beam coming down from the zenith of the heavens through your body, down to the earth's center, straightening your posture, connecting you to the earth.

If you're in a building rather than outdoors, bear in mind that the building is connected to the earth; you are connected to the earth. Feel that connection. Think of the earth as an enormous battery of *ki*; the more firmly your feet are connected to the earth, the more *ki* is available to you.

Close your eyes and notice if your weight is distributed evenly between your left and right feet. Move very subtly. Check to see that your weight is distributed evenly between your heels and the balls of your feet. Your knees are not locked and not bent, and you are becoming aware of the soles of your feet warming the surface beneath them and the surface beneath them warming your feet.

Now move your head gently from side to side and from front to back, making sure it's upright and balanced evenly on your trunk. Relax your neck, throat, mouth, jaw, and tongue. Relax your cheeks, temples, eyes, forehead; your entire scalp.

With a sharp intake of breath through your nostrils, raise and tighten your shoulders; then, with a full, relaxed exhalation through your mouth, let your shoulders melt softly and warmly downward. Let this soft, warm melting continue all the way down your body—front, back, and sides—relaxing all of you. Feel your hands becoming warm and heavy. Be aware of the loving embrace of gravity that holds you to the earth and the earth to you.

Give special attention to your back, an area we tend to ignore. Imagine sensing what's behind you without opening your eyes and turning to look around.

Get in touch again with your breathing, inhaling through the nostrils and exhaling through the mouth. Let each breath start in the abdomen and then move up to the chest. After two full breaths, open your eyes, letting your gaze remain soft and relaxed. Note that with soft eyes you can see objects on the periphery of your vision almost as clearly as those directly ahead. Maintaining soft eyes and letting your arms relax completely, begin rotating your body at the hips—left, right, left, right. Note that your relaxed arms will simply flop against your body at the end of each rotation. After a few of these, stop the rotations and shake out your hands, letting your wrists remain totally limp. Then open your fingers wide. Sense the flow of *ki* through your entire body; imagine it shooting out of your fingertips.

Before you start walking, slap yourself two or three times just beneath your hip bones. Then reach around behind you and tap the small of your back with the back of your fist. The idea here is to bring your attention to and energize these often ignored areas and make sure they're fully engaged in the process of walking. Again check your posture, which should be upright but not strained; you'll work your way into an improved posture gradually.

Put your attention on your center and stride out with high spirits and clear purpose. Breathe naturally and generously. Feel your feet on the surface beneath you, your arms swinging easily, your hands neither clenched nor held open rigidly but relaxed, with fingers slightly and gracefully curved. As each arm swings forward, the lower arm moves a little more than the upper arm, but make sure that the lower arm doesn't break at the elbow in an exaggerated fashion. In normal walking, this is wasted motion. (Race walking, with lower arms held at a fixed angle with upper arms, is another matter, using different vectors of motion.)

Set a comfortable, flowing stride, with legs swinging forward like pendulums, not thrusting at the ground like pistons. Check to see that every muscle in your body that isn't being used is completely relaxed. Bear in mind that "relaxed" doesn't mean limp. Avoid unnecessarily activating any muscle. Check especially for any tension in your back, chest, shoulders, neck, and, perhaps most important of all, face. You may recall seeing photographs of sprinters of past times grimacing in agony as they approached the finish line. Today's runners are coached to relax their faces; tightening the facial muscles accomplishes nothing and wastes energy. Even when you're walking quite briskly, aim for a pleasant, confident facial expression; it takes more muscles to frown than to smile.

Once you've established your stride, become increasingly

aware of your center, that essential point an inch or two beneath your navel. Think of your center moving forward easily through space. Consider your center rather than your chest, shoulders, or head as the focal point of your motion, your power. Widen your attention to include your hips and the small of your back, also important in the creation of seemingly effortless power. Hold this awareness and, at the same time, become exquisitely aware of the soles of your feet and their rounded, sensuous motion from heel to toe on the surface beneath you as they propel you across the earth.

Now, without compromising your upright posture, lower your center ever so slightly. This will bring your body physically closer to the surface on which you're walking by only a half inch or even less. But psychologically you'll feel and act as if you are considerably closer to the ground and thus considerably more stable and powerful. In addition, each foot will stay in contact with the ground a little longer than before and thus add a small but not inconsiderable length to your stride. This "getting down," this increased contact with the surface beneath you, is an essential element for success, not only in aikido but in all physical activities that involve walking or running.

Check your *zanshin*. It's not a question of constantly and compulsively looking around you but rather remaining aware of your surroundings in an appropriate way. Then, too, with soft eyes, your peripheral vision is significantly increased. *Zanshin* isn't merely a technique. It's a way of being alert and fully alive in the world. Walking is a good time for *zanshin*.

Changing Context in Walking

The basic aikido walk can be enhanced through the use of the imagination. Each of the following exercises involves a joining of mental imaging with the physical act of walking. You might try any of them that appeal to you—or make up imaging exercises of your own.

Walking through eternity. Set aside a five- to ten-minute period during your walk. Imagine that the way you walk during that period is the way you will be walking through all of eternity. This will encourage you to choose the way you will be walking through eternity by walking that way now. During the first part of the exercise, bring to mind all the things about your walk that you want to change. You might say to yourself, for example, any of the following, or whatever applies to you:

"If I'm walking with high shoulders now, I'll be walking with high shoulders through all of eternity. I can choose to change that now."

"If I'm walking with my head thrust forward now, my head will be thrust forward through all of eternity. I can choose to change that now."

"If I'm taking shallow breaths, I'll be taking shallow breaths through all of eternity. I can choose to change that now."

"If I'm walking with an unpleasant expression on my face, I'll have an unpleasant expression on my face for all of eternity. I can choose to change that now."

"If I'm bored now, I'll be bored through all of eternity. I can choose to change that now."

After going through all of the negative factors about your walk that you'd like to change and doing your best to change them, start making positive statements to yourself. For example:

"If I'm walking from center with full awareness on the soles of my feet, I'll be walking from center with full awareness on the soles of my feet through all of eternity!"

"If my breathing is relaxed and generous now, it will be relaxed and generous through all of eternity!"

"If my arms are swinging naturally and efficiently now, they'll be swinging naturally and efficiently through all of eternity!"

"If my posture is upright and supple, it will be upright and supple through all of eternity!"

"If I feel radiant and fully alive now, I'll be radiant and fully alive through all of eternity!"

From two-four to waltz time. Three rhythms for walking. Some people find themselves mentally humming a tune as they walk. Others move to a certain inner rhythm. Soldiers the world over march to a four-beat "*Hup*-two-three-four." Here's a sequence of three inner rhythms for your walk. Each has its own characteristic pulse. These rhythms aren't meant to make you accent any step physically; you should continue to stride evenly. The idea here is simply to *think* these rhythms as you walk, then notice what happens.

Start your walk with a count of *one-two*: left-right, left-right, *one-two*, *one-two*. Let this inner rhythm represent the *fact* of existence. One of the greatest philosophical riddles is simply that we exist, the world exists, the universe exists. You might consider this elemental and profound mystery while you stay with the straightforward, affirmative count of *one-two* for the first two or three minutes of your walk, noticing how you feel.

Then, without changing the tempo or length of your stride, shift to the familiar count of *one-two-three-four* This doesn't have to be militaristic. Let it be whatever it is, and let it represent the *form* of existence. While walking to this rhythm, consider that existence has form, that the universe is in the business of creating ever more complex forms, from atoms to human beings. Stay with the count of four for about five minutes, noting how you are walking, how you feel.

Again without changing the tempo or length of your stride, shift to the rhythm of the waltz: *one-two-three, one-two-three*. Note that the first beat now comes on alternate feet. Let this rhythm represent the *radiance* of existence. Consider the fact that all of what we call matter, in its simplest and most complex forms, radiates waves of electromagnetic energy. You are, literally, radiant.

Stay with this lively, ebullient rhythm for the remainder of your walk. Notice how you're walking, how you feel. Most people find that, after starting out with a two-count then going to a four-count, the waltz tempo gives them a lift, makes walking easier and more joyful. The same sequence can be used to good effect while running. Try out these and any other rhythms you wish and choose the one that's best for you.

Hill walking: Holding the tempo, changing the length of your stride. This way of walking is a favorite with experienced hikers and is especially helpful when hiking hilly country while carrying a pack. Set the tempo of your stride while walking on level ground. When your walk starts sloping upward, maintain the same tempo but shorten your stride. Should the slope become even steeper, make your stride even shorter—but maintain the same tempo. This is analogous to shifting or having your automatic transmission shift to a lower gear for uphill driving.

When you come to a slight downhill grade, you can slightly lengthen your stride. But take care. When the grade becomes too steep for comfort and safety using a longer stride, begin shortening it—just as you would put your car in a lower gear to descend steep hills. This practice not only increases your walking efficiency, but also, through the maintenance of a steady beat, produces a soothing, hypnotic quality on long walks or hikes.

Sailing on a wind of ki. Before starting to walk, tap your back a bit harder than usual with the back of your fist. Better, if you have a companion, take turns slapping each other's back all the way from the shoulders down to just below the waist. Inform your partner how hard you want to be slapped. The idea here is to heighten awareness of your back.

Now imagine there's a strong wind of *ki* blowing down the sidewalk or trail you're going to be walking on in just the direction you're going. When you begin walking, imagine that you're being pushed along by this *ki* wind. *Feel* the wind on your back. No need to lean forward in a struggle to keep going. Lean back very slightly into it. Let it push you. Let it carry you along.

Typically, this image increases the speed and ease of any walk. I explained sailing on a wind of *ki* to a neophyte hiker during one rather long hike. In an amazingly short time, he was a half mile ahead of us. When we caught up to him, he told us he hadn't been aware of how fast he was going.

Creating a field of positive energy. Aikido is an optimistic martial art, an art based on love and the loving protection of all beings. What better time to express this optimism and love than on a walk. Centered, grounded, graceful, confident walking can be said to create a field of energy that might well gladden the heart of anyone you encounter. I'm not suggesting here that you flash a big smile or sing out a greeting to people you pass unless it's appropriate. Just the way you walk can speak for itself.

"If I love the world as it is," writes the novelist Petru Dumitriu, "I am already changing it: a first fragment of the world has been changed, and that is my own heart." Let me add that if your heart changes for the better and you express it by the way you walk, there's a good chance that the hearts of those you encounter will change as well.

CHAPTER 16

Protecting the Attacker

It was a coffee break and one of my students named Lari was strolling along on a sidewalk near the computer store where he worked in Santa Rosa, a small city in northern California, when someone grabbed him from behind. He felt an arm around his neck and cool metal pressed near his jugular vein. Oh, it's just Peter playing his games again, Lari thought. His fellow student had playfully assaulted him from behind in a supermarket on more than one occasion to see how he would react.

Lari casually performed a technique that he, like all long-time aikido students, had practiced hundreds of times. He grasped the hand that held whatever metal object it was and, instead of struggling to push it away from him, pulled it tighter against his upper chest and then, still holding the hand in a specific, well-practiced grip, slipped his head down and in a turning motion escaped underneath the assailant's armpit, brushing his glasses off in the process. The move ended with Lari facing his assailant and holding his hand in a powerful wrist lock called a *sankyo*.

To Lari's surprise and horror, it wasn't Peter. It was a scruffy-looking man holding a knife. The knife was real.

What should he do? He had total control; the choice was his. At age fourteen, Lari had started practicing striking and kicking arts. Over the years he had earned black belts in two different forms of these arts. Had he not taken up aikido, he would have known just what to do. "I would have wasted him." But aikido's founder had said, "Protect your attacker." At that moment, holding his assailant in a *sankyo*, Lari was struck by a serious case of cognitive dissonance.

He took the man's knife away and threw it into a nearby bed of ivy. "I'm going to let you go this time," he said, releasing his assailant's hand. "Why don't you help me find my glasses?" The man picked up something, put it in a large bag, and started walking away as fast as he could.

At this point, Lari realized that the assailant had probably taken his $600 glasses with titanium frames. He ran after him, pushed him hard from behind on one shoulder, and began loudly demanding his glasses. The man claimed he didn't have them.

"Well, if you don't," Lari insisted, "the least you can do is come back and help me look for them."

From Lari's viewpoint, the situation was getting weirder by the moment. But more weirdness was still to come in the form of two police officers on bicycles who had been called by someone witnessing the argument from a nearby office window. At first, the police were inclined to arrest Lari but finally got the picture, especially when they found Lari's glasses in the man's bag. They took the assailant to jail and got Lari's story on a police report.

Shortly after that Lari phoned me at home and told me what had happened. He seemed greatly upset, not about the attack, but about how he had handled it. "Did I do the right thing?" he kept asking me. He wondered if, because of his aikido training, he would now be unable to "waste" someone who seriously threatened him in the future. I said that handling street attacks was a tricky business, but that this time everything seemed to have worked out. He had done a nice knife take-away technique, he wasn't hurt, and the attacker wasn't hurt. Probably he should have held the man for the police in the first place; still, the attacker had ended up in jail, where he belonged.

"Don't worry about it, Lari," I said. "You did fine."

Later, in court, the prosecutor wanted Lari to file charges, but he refused.

A Poignant Choice

Of all aikido's teachings, "protect the attacker" is probably the most radical and paradoxical. In a sense, it follows Jesus' saying that we should love our enemies, but it doesn't involve turning the other cheek. To the contrary, the moves of aikido, at best, protect both the one attacked and, insofar as it's possible, the attacker.

On the training mat, the safety of the attacker, the *uke*, can be assured, but only through the care and skill, the unspoken agreement, of all involved. While aikido may look dancelike, it is by no means a mere dance. The very act of attacking creates openings in the *uke*'s defense. Should the one attacked, the *nage*, oppose the attack, pushing back or striking back as is often the case in the nonaikido world, the *uke* could very quickly cover up his or her openings. But aikido's *entering* and *blending* moves leave the *uke* with nothing to fight, no opposition, and the *uke*'s openings tend to multiply. To say it another way, every skillful blend *creates* openings in the attacker.

The experienced *nage*, needless to say, sees these openings clearly and knows it would be possible to administer blows, kicks, foot sweeps, or damaging joint locks. At this point, however, the *nage* chooses to avoid doing anything that would hurt the *uke* and, instead, resorts to control techniques (as Lari did with his attacker) or throws that the *uke* can safely handle. Working with inexperienced students, teachers and advanced students administer control techniques slowly and gently and are careful not to put the newer students into a fall they can't handle.

As students become more advanced, they learn to attack all-out and take spectacular falls safely. A teacher knows who among his or her students can handle high-level training and will sometimes motion to one of them who loves to fly to rush in with, say, a hard chop aimed at the side of the head. Moving in and slightly off-line at the last split second, the teacher avoids the blow and uses its power to help launch the student in flight so that he or she lands with a graceful roll ten or twelve feet away. Such a fall by one who has never trained could result in serious injury or death.

With advanced as well as inexperienced *ukes*, the aikidoist *chooses* again and again, perhaps a hundred times or more in one class, *not* to harm his or her attacker *even though the opportunity to harm is present in almost every case*. If aikido were merely a dance, this choice to protect the attacker would be moot, and the art itself not nearly so poignant.

Needless to say, some who call themselves aikidoists use the art to feed their ego, playing the old game of asserting dominance through unnecessary and inappropriate force. By and large, however, the people who have chosen to train in this demanding art provide ego-free attacks when it's their turn to be *ukes* and protect their attackers when it's their turn to be *nages*.

"A Very Strict Love"

Off the mat, the dedicated aikidoist never starts a fight, seeks to avoid fights, endeavors to defuse fights. Simply by being balanced and centered and understanding the viewpoints of others, the aikidoist rarely gets into situations that would lead to physical violence. Should such violence occur, the aikidoist ideally tries to control the attacker with as little harm to him or her as possible.

One of my students named Chuck worked part-time, generally on weekends, in the psychiatric emergency room of a major urban hospital. Psychosis, often combined with a drug reaction, produced extremely violent tendencies in some of those brought in. After seeing Chuck deal with one particularly violent case, emergency-room personnel began calling

on him in all such cases, even those that would normally require several people to handle. His biggest problem was sub-
duing the violent patients without hurting them or letting
them hurt themselves. Chuck told me of one highly agitated
patient who kept struggling after he had pinned him, face-
down, with an armlock.

"You're breaking my arm," the patient kept screaming.

"Correction," Chuck said calmly. "*I'm* not breaking your
arm. You're *nearly* breaking your arm."

Aikido techniques proved highly effective against these
psychiatric patients' wild attacks. But Chuck was not totally
unscathed, suffering a few minor injuries himself in these encounters. Eventually, sickened by so much negative energy
and drug-related pathology, Chuck left this line of work.

It's a mistake in any case to think that aikido or any other
martial art can make you invincible. Once violence breaks
out, many unforeseeable and unfortunate things can happen. More than most people, well-trained aikidoists understand this and know that the best self-defense lies in not
letting violence happen in the first place. But they also know
that sometimes, despite all efforts to prevent them, vicious,
life-threatening attacks do occur.

In such cases, aikidoists are not expected to protect the
attacker at the expense of their own lives or the lives of others. In the words of Saotome Sensei: "Love of the enemy is a
very strict love. Sometimes, for the protection of others, that
love means destruction.   Society must be protected. The
rights of the individual and of individuality must be protected. The weak and the children must be protected. But

personal ego cannot be involved. Group or national ego cannot be involved."

A Possibility to Be Realized

Protecting the attacker applies to verbal as well as physical attacks. While there are verbal attacks so vicious, so degrading of human values that they must be forcefully struck down, it's counterproductive to use any word or action intended to devastate an attacker. Violence, whether physical or verbal, begets violence. Verbal violence, doctrinal violence, can lead to physical violence. Look at the results of interfamily feuds or ethnic struggles in which one side ravages the other, only to face revenge and retribution the next day, next year, next generation, next century. We have seen conflicts that last for hundreds of years and rob participants of their essential humanity to such an extent that they casually torture, rape, and kill whole families in the name of "ethnic cleansing."

Mitsugi Saotome quotes aikido's founder as saying, "True victory is not defeating an enemy. True victory gives love and changes the enemy's heart." Saotome Sensei goes on to explain, "O Sensei's great *satori* was the realization that love is true power, the application of the wisdom of God, not the narrow application of human strength. The great spiritual teachers have always taught that you must love your enemy; this is the highest love.   The most important point of *budo* [martial] training is to understand the enemy. If you understand, you cannot hate. Only in this way can you discover the true path of harmony."

To view a situation from an attacker's viewpoint while remaining centered and balanced can lead to seemingly miraculous outcomes. To go a step further, not only blending with and understanding the attacker but also, when possible, protecting him or her from harm, might seem the occupation of a saint, but it is actually a practical action that in most cases brings benefits to both parties.

I find it very sad, as I've said, that there are so few models of this behavior available in our culture. The glorification of ego-driven violence, torture, taunting, bullying, destruction, and physical and mental abuse of every conceivable stripe continues to escalate in our entertainment media. By the time our children come of age, they've witnessed many thousands of episodes of these types of behavior. Those who produce it argue that children can tell the difference between what happens on the screen and what happens in real life. They're right; there is a difference. What happens on the screen is far more vivid, more immediate, more compelling, and more appealing than the same sort of behaviors would be in real life.

The appeal of this kind of material to those who produce it is understandable. They want to attract an audience; they seek drama. And the spectacle of two men beating each other is superficially more dramatic than that of two men peacefully working out their differences. And it requires far less directing and acting ability.

We can only hope that the horrors on the screen will reach a point of saturation and that audiences will tire of the manipulations involved. Or, better, that those who produce our entertainment will gain the skill, and the courage, to trust the profound and poignant drama inherent in the refusal of conflict or its transformation into harmony.

But it's not just the entertainment media that can create models of behaviors that are both strong and loving. Every parent, teacher, school administrator, minister, elected official—actually, all of us—can model and encourage behaviors that promote love and understanding, even behaviors that protect rather than destroy attackers. It remains a possibility to be realized. It could change the way we live.

CHAPTER 17

The Wages of Optimism

A ikido is the most optimistic of martial arts. What other form of self-defense would welcome the attacker, love the attacker, and even *protect* the attacker? The words that have come down to us from our founder, Morihei Ueshiba, are just about as far removed from pessimism as I can imagine.

I am never defeated, however fast the opponent may attack. It is not because my technique is faster than that of the attacker. It is not a question of speed. The fight is finished before it is begun.

Aikido is nonresistance. As it is nonresistance, it is always victorious.

This is not mere theory. You practice it. Then you will accept the great power of oneness with nature.

When anybody asks if my aiki *budo* [martial art] principles are taken from religion, I say, "No, my true *budo* principles enlighten religions and lead *them* to completion.

There are neither opponents nor enemies for true *budo*. True *budo* is to be one with the universe; that is, to be united with the center of the universe.

Aikido is not a technique to fight with or defeat the opponent. It is the way to reconcile the world and make human beings one family.

Consider a common view of the optimist: a shallow, insipid fool, one who refuses to acknowledge the pain and grief and suffering that has dogged our steps from the beginning of history, one who looks at the world through rose-colored glasses, one who doesn't know what the score is. The word itself brings to mind such characters as the muddle-headed Dr. Pangloss in Voltaire's *Candide*, who dances through life repeating a phrase coined by the philosopher Leibniz: "All is for the best in this best of all possible worlds."

Even more ridiculous is Dr. Pangloss's literary descendant, Pollyanna. Created by novelist Eleanor H. Porter in 1913, this sweet and sappy little girl meets up with one misfortune after another. But no problem: Her father, before dying and leaving her an orphan, taught her the "glad game." Whatever happens, however dreadful it might be, Pollyanna finds something to be glad about. When a man breaks his leg, for example, she tells him he should be glad he broke only one leg rather than two. The book was an enormous success.

Glad Clubs were formed all over the world. More Pollyanna books followed from Ms. Porter's pen and, after her death, from the pens of others. Then there were the movies, one in 1920 starring Mary Pickford, another in 1960 starring Hayley Mills.

Actually, the Pollyanna character isn't a true optimist, but rather a person who reacts to misfortune in a stereotypical and quite limited manner. The true optimist is someone who tends to operate on the assumption that things will work out positively; the true pessimist takes the opposing point of view. At best, the true optimist *acts* on his or her assumption of positive outcomes, but not in denial of negative factors. Nonetheless, Pollyanna's enduring legacy is the creation of a new word, *pollyanna*, in English and in other languages, a term of derision applied to anyone who takes an optimistic point of view.

But there's more than that to the relatively low status of optimism among the cognoscenti. Tragedy appears to have a long-term leasehold on what is most profound in our view of the human condition. In darkness, there is a depth that tends to diminish in the light. The auteurs of film noir seem formidable, heavy, while the makers of happy movies are, well, *lite.* Hope makes you vulnerable while existential despair is both fashionable and safe. The pessimist might not be happy but is never disappointed. When things go wrong he or she says, "I told you so. I knew all along it wouldn't work." To sum it up, optimism is uncool.

Optimism Versus Pessimism

Uncool or not, however, optimists tend to be more successful, happier, healthier, and longer-lived than pessimists. Hundreds of studies during the past twenty-five years have demonstrated that even people who are *unrealistically* optimistic fare better in life than do *realistic* pessimists. You might wonder if the people in the studies are optimistic simply *because* they're successful, happy, and healthy. But many of these studies are longitudinal, that is, they follow the people being studied over a period of time to see how they fare, having started out as either optimists or pessimists.

One study, for example, focused on ninety-nine Harvard students, all of whom were examined and given medical tests in 1946 at age twenty-five and found to be in good health. Every five years for the next thirty-five years, they were again examined and tested. Using in-depth interviews about difficult wartime experiences written at the beginning of the study, researchers rated the students as optimistic or pessimistic. There wasn't much difference in the health of the two groups for about ten years. Then, between ages thirty-five and forty, the health of the pessimists began worsening compared to that of the optimists. The difference became significantly greater between ages forty and forty-five.

A great deal of research over the years has also shown that optimists fare better than pessimists during and after coronary bypass surgery and live longer with HIV. Even susceptibility to the common cold seems to be associated with pessimistic ways of thinking and talking. And a 1998 study has shown that healthy people under considerable stress who are optimists increase the power of their immune system far more than do healthy pessimists under the same stress.

Other studies suggest that optimists persevere where pessimists don't, make more successful salespeople, bounce back more quickly after failures, do better in school and in sports, are more likely to win political races, and are less likely than pessimists to become depressed. Clearly, pessimism has a role in human life, or it wouldn't have persisted through eons of evolution. Pessimists tend to view matters, especially those dealing with the possible failure of projects, more realistically than do optimists. Psychologist Martin Seligman, a leader in the study of optimism, believes that a corporation needs optimists as researchers and developers, planners, and marketers. But there is a role for pessimists as CPAs, business administrators, safety engineers, and chief financial officers.

Seligman and others in the field of cognitive-behavioral psychology believe that optimism can be learned by changing lifelong habits of thought; more specifically, by adopting better ways of explaining bad events. According to Seligman, the pessimist's "explanatory style" is personal ("It's my fault"), permanent ("It's always going to be like this"), and pervasive ("It's going to undermine every aspect of my life").

The optimist's way of explaining bad events is by making them external rather than personal ("I dropped the ball because the sun got in my eyes"), temporary rather than permanent ("It was a fluke. I rarely miss"), and specific rather than pervasive ("It had no effect on the rest of my play").

In explaining *good* events, the roles are reversed. The pessimist tends to explain good things by viewing them as external ("A big sale fell into my lap today"), temporary ("Nothing this easy could ever happen again"), and specific ("This guy was one of those rare idiots who doesn't know what he's doing"). The optimist tends to explain them as personal ("I made a great sale today"), permanent ("I'm always running into the right client"), and pervasive ("Whatever happens, it seems I just can't miss").

Cognitive-behavioral therapists teach their clients the skills of optimism. Exercises are provided that show the *consequences* of optimistic vs. pessimistic ways of thinking about adversity, and through these exercises the value of optimism is realized. Best of all, clients are asked to actually practice their new ways of thinking and talking during their daily lives.

Saying Yes to Life

Optimism, let it be said, doesn't guarantee good health and success in life, but it clearly increases your odds in achieving them. Sadly, there are people so strongly committed to the negative outlook that they would rather risk ill health and failure than relinquish their views, people who would rather be right than be happy. We all know such people. And if you desire to make a shift in your habits of thought from the negative to the positive, there's no one approved way to do so. Ultimately, it comes down to a matter of choice. Do you really *want* to say yes to life, not merely for the extrinsic rewards it might bring but basically for its own sake?

As for me, I'm not always an optimistic person. I have my

times of pessimism and doubt. But I have no doubt whatsoever that "yes" is the signpost I want to follow into the future. Even in my lowest moments, I've never lost that faith. Just as a certain naïveté is the prerequisite to all learning, a certain optimism is the prerequisite to all action. And if our destiny on this planet is to learn, it is not so much our obligation as our privilege to act on that learning.

The matter of optimism vs. pessimism is more complex, more resistant to definition than the system devised by the cognitive-bahaviorist psychologist would have it. All systems are necessarily incomplete; still, we need them to help focus our understanding. Beyond any system, however, stands the age-old ability of our species to hope for something better and act on that hope, even when all seems lost, even on the approach of death.

CHAPTER 18

The Primacy of Play

It was late in the afternoon on one of those golden days that grace the end of summer in northern California. Annie and I had hiked to one of our favorite spots on Mt. Tamalpais, an area marked "wooded knoll" on our trail map. The sky was clear, the air balmy with a gentle, steady breeze that whispered quietly of autumn. We sat on the edge of a small thicket of trees for a while looking some fifteen hundred feet down at the line of breakers tracing the long, gracious curve of Stinson Beach. It was getting late, so we started back to where we had parked our car, about two miles away. The trail took us out over a large area of rounded slopes covered with grasses turned golden by the heat of summer, now burnished to a deeper gold by the setting sun. To the north, the land sloped down from us all the way to the Pacific. To the east, it sloped upward about five hundred feet, undulating like the haunches of some enormous living thing.

In all this vastness, there was not a human being in sight. Ahead of us, the trail swerved around a small knoll. As we approached the knoll, we were brought to a halt by an amazing sight.

Just in front of the knoll, facing the breeze, were five swallows. Their wings were open but not moving, nor were the birds themselves moving. The five of them were absolutely motionless, frozen in space. It was as if they were mounted on invisible rods. Very cautiously, we went closer. Still they didn't move, not even an inch, in relation to the earth. Finally, one of them seemed to slip slightly down and backward. Immediately, beating its wings, it circled around and approached the line of swallows from behind, eased into position, made a few precise corrections, and again became utterly motionless.

It was an aeronautical feat involving an exquisite balance of forces. There in front of the knoll, the air from the breeze was being forced slightly upward so that the birds could be gliding slightly down in relation to the air while remaining at precisely the same height in relation to the earth. But they would also have to maintain the exact speed through the air that would keep them from slipping even a hair fore and aft and do this without moving their wings. In addition, to keep themselves from drifting right or left, they would have to line themselves up exactly into the wind with an accuracy hard to imagine. Now and then, one or another of them would lose its amazingly precise point of balance, but it would quickly circle around to resume its place.

We stood transfixed, afraid to move. A question from William Blake echoed in my consciousness:

How do you know but ev'ry Bird that cuts the airy way,
Is an immense world of delight, clos'd by your senses five?

But what were these swallows really doing? Behavioral biologists will go to any lengths to explain how everything an animal does serves a purpose, and that purpose is to enhance its survival and to pass on its genes to the next generation. When lion cubs attack each other with mock cuffs and bites, we all agree that they are playing. The biologists tell us, however, that they play only to prepare themselves for their work as adult predators.

Yes, that's one way of saying it. But what if any, is the difference between "work" and "play"? And even if there is a clear difference, what work were the birds on Mt. Tam preparing for? There are certain raptors that hover motionless while searching the ground for prey, but swallows are not hovering birds. They seek insects with swift, darting flight. No insects were coming their way on the breeze. Their beaks never opened.

They were playing.

What are we doing in the dojo? We might have first come to aikido for self-defense or fitness or balance. But after a few months these considerations fade away. We are doing it, with all that it entails—strenuous exertion, pain, close calls, occasional injury, along with years and years of what you might call "hard work"—for the sheer delight of it.

We are playing.

Maximizing the Play

In his inspired, evocative book, *Homo Ludens: A Study of the Play Element in Culture,* the Dutch philosopher Johan Huizinga shows how what we call play operates in music and poetry, war and law, ritual and sacrifice, courtship and fashion, art and philosophy—in practically every aspect of life. He argues that other things can be explained in terms of play, but that play, being primordial, can't be explained in terms of other things. Play precedes culture. It extends beyond the rational, beyond abstraction, beyond matter. Play, in short, is irreducible.

Let's simply say that play is whatever absorbs us fully, whatever creates purpose and order, whatever involves us in as much meaningful interaction as is possible. In our best games, there's always a certain edge to that interaction, a fine balance between victory and defeat. We like close calls, tight races. In baseball, for example, second base is exactly ninety feet from first base. Were the bases five feet closer together, almost every runner would be able to steal second. Were they five feet farther apart, hardly any runner would make it. We have chosen the precise distance that creates the greatest chance of a close call. When a good base runner makes it to first base, the pulses of all those involved—players, spectators in the stands, members of the television audience—quicken. Colors become warmer, more vivid. A delicious suspense heightens all our senses. The player on first base takes off for second. The catcher stands and fires the ball, and time slows down as the runner slides into second only a hairsbreadth before the ball.

Why are we so fascinated with the exquisite balance of forces, with close calls, near brushes with disaster in our games? Why have we arranged our play to maximize these factors? Perhaps it's because that's the way it is and has been since the birth of time and space, a defining characteristic of all existence. Consider what goes on within our own bodies: the fine and sometimes precarious balance between heat and cold, glucose and insulin; the sympathetic and parasympathetic nervous systems, positive and negative charges across the cell membrane. Note the play involved in the vast armies of immune cells searching out enemies, engaging in epic, life-and-death contests; the urgent messages cascading through networks of nerve fibres; oscillations dancing in the brain to create virtual switchboards that last only seconds; neuro-peptides swimming through veins and arteries to solace the heart and hearten the gut; red blood cells dying, others being born, two and a half million of them every second.

"One's body," aikido's founder said again and again, never tiring of the words, "is a miniature universe." The evolution of the physical universe has involved the same sorts of inter-actions as those within the body; the almost impossibly deli-cate balances of forces, close calls, near brushes with disaster. No wonder, then, that our best myths and dramas as well as our best games involve precarious moments of suspense dur-ing which all seem lost and then, somehow, against all odds, is saved. Could it be that the universe itself is a vast con-spiracy to maximize play?

If so, how sad it is, as we leave childhood behind, that we are taught in countless explicit and implicit ways to work hard rather than to play joyfully. We find ourselves imprisoned on an iron rack of contingencies. We are taught to do one thing only to achieve another thing. Study hard so that you'll get good grades. Get good grades so that you can get into a good college. Get into a good college so that you'll get a good job. Get a good job and work hard so that you can have the good things in life. By the time you get the "good things," however, you can barely remember how to play.

Aikido summons all of us, whether we do aikido or not, to play and keep playing from childhood to old age, to seek out the possibilities of play in every aspect of living—in what we call "work," in love and sex, in relationships with family and friends, even in taking a walk around the block.

The strange thing is that when we approach an activity in the spirit of play—that is, fully, joyfully, and primarily for its own sake—we are likely to achieve not only the greatest happiness but also the best results, the most enduring success.

CHAPTER 19

The Magical Marriage of Practice and Play

If the aikido training mat is the world, it's the world under a magnifying glass. Subtle personality quirks are made large and clear. Hidden agendas come quickly to light. Every attempt at overreaching is revealed in sharp relief. After you've been doing the art for a while, it's amazing how much you can learn about people simply by how they grasp your wrist or by their reaction when you grasp theirs. Episodes of childhood trauma loudly announce themselves by the way a person's head shrinks back and to the side as a partner's hand comes near. Inability to express emotions proclaims itself in bodily rigidity. Fear of touch or of intimacy, unless remedied, can eventually drive one from the mat; aikido is a tactile, intimate art.

Broader cultural proclivities also pop up to glare at you like gargoyles when you open an aikido school. Perhaps the most striking of these is the urgent desire in this culture for quick results with a minimum of effort, along with a concomitant distaste for any long-term path of practice that yields slow results. What we call "mastery" can be defined as that mysterious process through which what is at first difficult or even impossible becomes easy and pleasurable through diligent, patient, long-term practice. Aikido, perhaps as much as any other human activity, reveals the reliable and seemingly miraculous transformative power of such practice. It also shows how doggedly we resist it. Nobody—I repeat *nobody*—is going to look good after only a few classes. Athletic prowess can help but is no guarantee. An Olympic gold medalist quit after three classes because he didn't like the feeling of making no discernible progress.

There's something especially endearing about brand-new aikido students in their shiny white uniforms, still stiff from lack of repeated washings. They are, in a way, our most valuable students; like babies, they represent our future. All of us, not only we the instructors but the experienced students as well, do what we can to ease their pathway into a challenging new skill. But, sadly, of those who first step onto the mat, less than fifty percent will be there a month later. Their reasons for quitting are many and varied. Still, certain character types emerge, and what we see under the magnifying glass of our training is generally true to one degree or another in other aspects of their lives.

The Dabbler and the Obsessive

There's the Dabbler who flits from one sport to another, from one job or one mate to another. The Dabbler loves the first fine flush of things, honeymoons, the shine of newness. Eyes gleaming, he or she approaches the instructor after class to say how wonderful it was, tells friends all about aikido, demonstrates techniques. At the first tentative spurt of "progress," the Dabbler's enthusiasm exceeds all bounds. When, inevitably, this upward spurt doesn't continue, the Dabbler become restless. Well, maybe aikido isn't right for me after all. It's too physical. Or too spiritual. Or too philosophical. So it's off to something new and different—t'ai chi or karate or golf or whatever. And if, as is generally the case, the Dabbler's pattern pervades all of his of her life, it's off to another job, another love relationship as well.

There's nothing wrong with trying out new things to see what's right for you. There are times in life for experimentation. But when dabbling becomes habitual, it can prevent any long-term journey of mastery.

The Obsessive is different. He or she comes into the dojo with an urgent mission. Energy so far forward that you can feel it ten feet away, the Obsessive asks the teacher, "How long will it take me to master aikido?" The teacher can only answer, "How long do you expect to live?" At the end of the first class, the Obsessive comes up to the desk. "What books or videotapes can I buy so I can learn faster? How about private lessons?" The teacher replies that books and tapes and private lessons don't really help until you've gained some feeling for the art in your body. At the end of the next class, the Obsessive asks, "Can I stay after class and practice? I'm going to get this technique right if it takes me all night." "Well, I've been doing aikido for nearly thirty years," the teacher replies, "and I've never gotten that technique exactly right."

When I encounter such a student, I do all I can to change his or her attitude. Just stay on the mat, I say. Keep coming to classes, stay in the present moment, enjoy your training. Progress will eventually come; if you keep practicing, it's inevitable. There's a pang in my heart. If this student's attitude doesn't change, I can be reasonably sure that he or she won't be around a month later.

All too often, the Obsessive drops out because of an injury. So much overreaching, so much forward energy, can lead to catastrophe—physical, psychological, relational, financial. As on the mat, so in the outside world. In the quest for "progress" at all costs, the Obsessive can be driven to cut corners, engage in illegal or hurtful behavior. In relationships, the extreme Obsessive, unwilling to take no for an answer, becomes a stalker.

Yes, there are times, on a tough deadline or in an emergency situation, when all of us are appropriately obsessive. Again, it's only when the behavior becomes habitual that it works against us.

The Dabbler and the Obsessive represent special character types that resist the path of mastery, but almost all of us are resistant to one degree or another. Learning any significant skill requires that, between spurts of apparent progress, we continue practicing diligently while seeming to make little or no progress. These plateaus can be quite long, especially when learning particularly difficult skills. In any case, the time we spend on plateaus is almost sure to be far longer than the time we spend making spurts of progress.

Mastery Versus the Quick Fix

There's a secret here, hidden from us by our restless desire for continual progress and our consumerist culture's false promise of fast, easy results: *Most learning occurs while we're on the plateau.*

You're just starting to learn tennis. Your instructor drops the ball for you to hit a simple forehand. Again and again you try it. You listen carefully to what your instructor says. You feel clumsy, out of sync. The ball goes into the net or over the fence or ricochets off the edge of the racket. Hours go by, days. You seem to be getting nowhere. Then one fine day everything is different. The ball sails over the net and into the green more often than not. Your stroke feels more natural. This simple forehand is beginning to seem easy.

"Ah, *at last!*" you think. "Now I'm really learning."

Wrong. You were learning while you were on the plateau, seeming to make no progress at all. This spurt upward toward mastery merely marked the moment when the results of your training "clicked in," when as is sometimes said, you got it into your muscle memory.

Enjoy the spurt but also enjoy the next plateau. And as you go on to learn more advanced aspects of tennis, or anything else beyond the simplest skills, there will surely be a next plateau and a next and a next. The point here is so obvious that I'm almost embarrassed to make it. Yet in the land of the quick fix it sometimes seems radical: To learn anything significant, to make any lasting change in yourself, you must be willing to spend *most* of your time on the plateau. Not only that, but to join those on the path of mastery, it's best to *love* the plateau, to take delight in regular practice not just for the extrinsic rewards it brings, but for its own sake.

Ever since I began planning a forty-page special section for *Esquire* on mastery, which appeared in the May 1987 issue, I've been studying, interviewing, corresponding with, or just talking to people considered to be masters in their fields. Their opinion is almost unanimous that diligent, high-quality, long-term practice is more important than talent. In most of these people, I've also discovered a fascination with and, yes, a love of practice, a willingness to keep on practicing even in the absence of apparent progress. Research studies back up the opinion of expert practitioners that while talent is important, practice is far more important as a factor in high-level performance.

With all that, our culture continues to bombard us with promises of fast, easy results and instant gratification. The cultural pressure in favor of the quick fix and against long-term practice and mastery is indeed ubiquitous and insidious. The vast majority of self-help books promise maximum results with minimum practice—instant enlightenment, overnight learning, total fitness in thirty minutes a week, management expertise in a minute. At a recent New Age fair, I ran across what might be the *sine qua non* of this genre, a small book entitled *God Made Easy*. Television commercials offer up a brave new world consisting entirely of climactic moments; there's no plateau. Such a world can be replicated—for a while—through the use of illegal drugs, which is disproportionately high in the United States. But legal drugs also play their part. Consider the bizarre phrase: "Fast, temporary relief."

It's inescapable. Movies and television dramas mimic MTV, playing up to the restlessness they help cultivate by cutting from scene to scene at intervals that keep getting shorter and shorter—new explosions, new titillations, new horrors every few seconds. Then there's the current epidemic of legalized gambling, which is not only a tax on the poor, but a brazen advertisement for instant, effortless riches for everyone. No need to practice. No plateau. And how about crime itself, an activity we glorify in countless overt and covert ways? How much practice and skill does it take to pull out a cheap handgun? You get fast results, but, as in most cases of the quick fix, the results are harmful to society as well as to the individual.

Here's a dilemma. Perhaps, at least in part, our national prosperity is dependent upon our restlessness, our manufactured desire for one quick fix after another, for experiences and consumer products that we don't need and, in a deeper sense, don't even want. Note that advertisers are becoming more and more blatant in their slash-and-burn campaigns to make us spend our credit cards to the limit. Ads appear in the most unlikely places: printed on the inside of frozen orange-juice cans, pasted on the fruits and vegetables we buy at the supermarket. Don't be surprised if someday a running-shoe emblem is embossed on the front teeth of a sports celebrity (for God knows how much money) so that it will show in television close-ups. But maybe I'm behind the curve. Maybe it's already been done.

How unfortunate if it turned out that we had to become ever more addicted to the quick-fix way of life in order to maintain what we call prosperity. Such a life brings no lasting satisfaction, only ephemeral sensations of pleasure followed quickly by dissatisfaction, sometimes despair, and always a restless desire for something else, something new, something *out there*.

Allure and Disillusionment

While the appeals are powerful, there are millions of people who have become disillusioned with the quick fix. People who have tried it all, the promises of instant gratification, wealth, health, weight loss, whatever. People who have found it doesn't work.

Some of us might also have attended those cathartic weekend workshops where we reveal our darkest secrets with strangers who give us the kind of approval and love we've never dreamed of, and we might have left feeling wide awake and fully alive. We might have succumbed to the allure of high-intensity spiritual or psychedelic experiences and might have left with vivid glimpses of the infinite and the eternal. Yes, the feelings are real, the glimpses encode aspects of spiritual truth. We are indeed transformed. But without some long-term practice that supports and renews that feeling and those glimpses, the transformation begins to fade. Within weeks it is gone.

Our own personal experiences with the failure of intense, short-term transformative sessions is partly what led Michael Murphy and me in 1992 to create a long-term program for realizing the potential of mind, body, heart, and soul. We called the program Integral Transformative Practice (ITP). It's *integral* in that it integrates mind, body, heart, and soul and also integrates the practice with the practitioner's daily life. It's *transformative* in that it aims for long-term, positive change. And it's a *practice* in that it entails long-term dedication to a nontrivial activity primarily for its own sake. A two-year experimental ITP class involving fifty participants yielded highly positive results, as reported in our book *The Life We Are Given*. Currently, there are some forty ITP groups practicing in the United States and overseas. (For further information, see the Appendix.)

We Are Always Practicing

Our work with ITP has led Murphy and me to the realization that all of us are constantly practicing and that practice isn't always deliberate. The problem is that so often, without our knowing it, we're practicing behaviors, ways of being that are not at all what we would consciously wish.

Say, for example, that a young boy frequently raises his shoulders as a way of warding off blows from abusive parents. With enough practice, the boy learns to keep his shoulders tense and high. When we meet him as an adult, we wonder how he is able to maintain such an unnatural posture. We should realize that he's had to master this difficult—and unfortunate—skill. He's *practiced* it.

Or maybe you're at a dinner party for eight where seven of the diners want to discuss positive proposals for the future. Whenever something positive comes up, however, the eighth diner intervenes: "No way! That'll never work. Can't you see?" He goes on to make objections A, B, and C. He continues devastating any positive proposal until all discourse ceases. You're annoyed and perhaps angry. Still, you can't help wondering how that eighth diner got so very good at being negative. You might stop to think that he's been practicing it for, say, forty years.

Many forms of therapy tend to neglect or entirely ignore the role of practice in human change. Insight therapies can be viewed as long-term practices, but just what are their patients practicing? They are learning to understand what in their past caused their neuroses, how the neuroses operate in their present life, and how to talk about it. They get very good at insight and are often brilliant in discussing psychological theory as it applies to their own cases. But rarely are they offered help in creating a program for *practicing* desirable feeling and behaviors. The increasing appeal of cognitive-behavioral therapies perhaps stems from the fact that they provide clients with programs to help them actually practice alternative ways of contextualizing and interacting.

Pills for the mind can be quite effective in correcting chemical imbalances that cause serious mental disorders. And they can reduce the paralyzing effects of anxiety or depression in "normal neurotics." But that's only a beginning.

Making any significant, long-term psychological change, whether getting back to normal or moving on toward extraordinary states of love, power, and joy, always involves some sort of long-term practice.

Reliable Magic

I mention these few examples to show how fully practice, whether deliberate or unconscious, pervades our lives. Still, it's not just the ubiquity of practice that makes it a crucial factor in human life, but also its truly incredible power to transform. In recent decades, we've probably been offered more substances and experiences reputed to yield immediate and extraordinary effects than at any period in human history. This includes crystals, pyramids, herbs, exotic diets, fasts, and drugs, plus short-term therapies and "trips" of every imaginable variety. And we've come to realize that none of these can guarantee significant, lasting results.

Ironically, it's what we would least think of as magical that provides truly magical results. If, with proper instruction, you should undertake a regimen of regular, diligent, patient practice primarily for its own sake rather than for immediate results, you are almost certain to experience significant positive change within a year. This is true whether you're practicing to play better tennis or to become a more loving person. Nearly all the participants in our ITP class realized significant and sometimes seemingly magical improvements across a wide spectrum of human functioning—greatly boosting strength, achieving a flow state at work, increasing empathy, reducing a percentage of body fat, experiencing mystical states. Improvements in overall vitality and health were especially noteworthy and in some cases—reversing cataracts, for example—beyond conventional medical explanation.

The Eternal Present

Beneath the remarkable efficacy of practice is the intrinsic joy it can bring. We tend to think of the word *routine* along with the word *boring*. Looking at it another way, however, we can see that it's the obsessive search for novelty that is the very essence of boredom. In the routine of a strong and beautiful practice, there is continual renewal and deep satisfaction.

A successful artist I know has told me of the great pleasure she finds simply in entering her studio at the same time in the morning five days a week, smelling the paint, taking her seat at the easel, arranging her brushes. "The routine is important to me. When I get started, there's a wonderful sense of well being. I like to feel myself plodding along. I specifically choose that word, *plod*. When it's going good, I feel 'this is the essential me.' It's the routine itself that feeds me. If I didn't do it, I'd be betraying the essential me."

It's been the same for me every one of the thousand times I've climbed the stairway to the dojo and opened the door. Standing there a moment, I bow respectfully and enter, caressed by the special ambience, the electric *presence* that permeates the space. No matter that I was feeling somewhat jangled from the day's hectic minutiae, I am immediately calmed and energized, my body tingling, my spirit replenished. I take off my shoes, check the desk and the bulletin board, go into the dressing room, change to my aikido garb. I love it all: the sameness, the reliability, the *routine*, along with the new developments that each class brings. I love to greet the students as they come in. I love watching them as they take to the mat. I love the cool, firm pressure of the mat on the soles of my feet, the ritual bows, the warm-up exercises, and then my heart pounding, my breath rushing as the training increases in speed and power.

Sometimes, when I first glance up at the clock, I'm surprised that an hour has passed, happy to realize that during that magic interval I've lived neither in the future nor in the past, but rather at the mysterious point of repose that exists in an entirely different realm: the eternal present.

But it's not necessary to be an artist or a practitioner of an Asian martial art to realize the pleasures of long-term practice. Even something as commonplace as gardening can be a practice if done not primarily to impress the neighbors or win prizes for one's roses, but for the sheer love of it, as an essential expression of one's soul. There's a paradox here. The person who gardens primarily for the love of it, as a practice, is the one who is likely to impress the neighbors and win prizes for his or her roses.

The same thing is true in many aspects of life: exercising, doing your finances, working around the house. On a visit, Marshall McLuhan insisted on washing the dishes after dinner. "It's my meditation," he told us.

Perhaps more important, what we call our work can be recontextualized as a practice. The key question again is whether you are doing it primarily for its own sake or primarily for its extrinsic rewards. This isn't always possible, but in more cases than you might imagine, it's a choice you can make.

A Happy Marriage

As you might have gathered, there's a striking similarity between practice and play. If play, as proposed in the preceding chapter, is whatever absorbs us fully, whatever creates purpose and order, whatever involves us in as much meaningful interaction as is possible, then almost every practice can be made into play, while play can be seen as sharing many of the characteristics of practice. Again, at best, both are done primarily for their own sakes; there's joy and satisfaction in the doing, not just in the results. When I told a fellow aikido instructor that I thought aikido should be fun, she replied, "I think it should be dead serious." But what is more dead serious than a child, or an adult, deeply engrossed in a game?

Finally, it is this feeling of being totally absorbed and entranced that joins play and practice in a marriage where both past and future fall away and we are privileged to exist, if only for a while, in the present moment. The greatest spiritual leaders tell us that this is the place where God is. It is also where the most efficient and ecstatic learning of every kind can happen. If the human destiny on this planet is to learn, then it is through the happy, magical marriage of practice and play that we can best realize that destiny.

CHAPTER 20

Under the Sword

When the samurai Kikushi was ordained a bodhisattva [one devoted to lifelong service], his master told him, "You must concentrate upon and consecrate yourself wholly to each day, as though a fire were raging in your hair."

In single combat, before the time of the gun, the medieval Japanese samurai was perhaps the most fearsome warrior ever known. The steel of his *katana* was exquisitely tempered and so sharp it could sever silk cloth that was simply dropped on its blade. He was superbly trained. His techniques involved lightning-fast strikes and parries; often, one or two strokes decided the battle. But perhaps what made him most fearsome of all was his absolute presence and clarity when he stood before his foe.

In the best of the samurai movies, there are likely to be scenes in which two samurai stand facing each other, swords raised, motionless, for one, two, perhaps even three minutes. Those who haven't studied Japanese swordsmanship might find themselves bored and restless during such scenes. Those who understand are riveted. They know that each of the combatants is waiting for the tiniest break in the *ki* of the other. The outcome of the battle is contained in those motionless moments. The break occurs, swords flash in the sunlight, and it's over.

Long and arduous training contributed to the samurai's presence and clarity in combat, but there was also another key factor: The samurai had to be totally free of considerations. If, for example, he was to think, "Why didn't I have my sword sharpened?" or "I should have settled my debt with Takeda-san," the break in *ki* would be fatal. The ultimate consideration is one's own death. For the thought "I might die" to creep into his consciousness would mean sure death. That's why the samurai was trained from earliest childhood to go into battle with no thought of either life or death. Being ready to die, he was more likely to live.

Bushido, the Way of the Warrior

In 1603, after many years of wars and uprisings, the leading Japanese warlords were unified under the Tokugawa Shogunate. There ensued a period of relative peace and isolation that lasted nearly 250 years. During the Tokugawa period, the samurai—men and women—turned the same highly focused clarity and intensity that had created great warriors into the creation of an exquisite artistry that permeated every aspect of their lives.

From the samurai class came the Noh drama, the tea ceremony, haiku poetry, traditional flower arranging, sumi brush painting, and much of the greatest ceramic art. There were still rigid class lines and special privileges for the samurai that would be anathema to our modern democratic sensibilities. But it can't be denied that the Japanese marriage of the martial spirit with the artistic spirit remains one of the highest achievements of any culture.

The Tokugawa period also saw the fullest flowering of *bushido*, the way of the warrior, a chivalric code somewhat like that of the medieval knights of England and Europe. At best, this code enjoined the samurai to uphold the virtues of loyalty, integrity, dignity, courtesy, courage, prudence, and benevolence. It entailed service to his *daimyo*, his warlord, and to the *kami*, the divine spirits he revered; the word *samurai* means "to serve."

Going Under the Sword

Aikido, as stated in the Introduction, is a radical reform of the samurai tradition, but it still owes much to the samurai spirit. Saotome Sensei tells of the time when O Sensei, then around fifty years old, was challenged by a superb swordmaster. The two of them walked into O Sensei's garden, the swordmaster carrying his highly polished sword, O Sensei empty-handed.

The sun flashed off the brightly polished steel as the *kendo* master moved into his *kamae* [stance], O Sensei standing quietly before him. And they stood. Sweat began to break on the *kendo* master's forehead, rolling down his cheeks like tears. It fell like a thousand prisms from the stained and glistening muscles of his powerfully developed forearms. And still they stood. O Sensei, calm and detached, aware but not waiting, only reflected the image of the man and the glittering steel before him. Five, seven, maybe ten minutes passed. Exhausted from the struggle of attempting to attack the universe, the *kendo* man surrendered. He had been unable to move. His acute sensitivity and perception had revealed no openings in O Sensei's defense.[1]

O Sensei had not, as some people thought, hypnotized his opponent through some secret Oriental technique. It was rather that his mind was pure and free of ego, revealing only harmony. In a sense, there was no one for the swordmaster to attack but himself.

In practicing sword take-aways, advanced aikido students must go under the sword as O Sensei did—though by no means with the intensity related in the above episode. Normally, we use a *bokken* (wooden sword) for these exercises. The *bokken*, it should be said, isn't a make-believe steel sword; it's a real wooden sword, capable of causing severe injury or death. Miyamoto Musashi, the greatest of samurai, chose the *bokken* for some of his most famous duels.

Two aikidoists stand facing each other, one with *bokken* raised, the other unarmed. The spacing is such that the aikidoist with the sword has to step forward in order to bring the sword down on the unarmed aikidoist's head. The unarmed aikidoist doesn't look at the sword or into the attacker's

[1]Mitsugi Saotome, *Aikido and the Harmony of Nature*, Shambhala, Boston, 1993, pp. 141–142.

eyes but rather looks with a soft gaze at the attacker's *hara*, his physical center. Only when the center moves does he or she step forward and slightly off the line of attack as the sword slashes down, barely missing its target. In this manner, the unarmed aikidoist ends up to the side of and very close to the attacker. From that position, he or she can grasp the hilt of the sword and/or the attacker's hands and, through various techniques, take the sword away.

While standing with raised sword, the attacker can try to make the unarmed aikidoist flinch and move prematurely by faking a strike or shouting. The essence of the exercise and its greatest joy comes from standing absolutely motionless until the attacker's center moves and the strike is already on its way. Sometimes the attacker waits a long while before actually attacking. During this electric interval, you have the opportunity of being totally in the present. Are you worried about credit-card debt or your housing situation? Under the sword, these worries tend to melt away. There is only the moment, and the moment can be delicious. Once the attacker's center moves and the sword starts down on you, there's the opportunity, not to stop time, but to open it up and examine its previously unrealized possibilities. Sometimes a second expands into what seems to be ten or perhaps even twenty seconds. You can wait quite a while and still have plenty of time to move calmly out of the way, enjoying the whistling sound as the sword goes past your ear a few inches away.

Playing this edge takes considerable practice and is not for the beginner. But in my workshops, especially those involving the Samurai Game™, I give nonaikidoists the chance to go under the sword in a carefully controlled situation. After having them practice the *entering/off the line* move for about a half hour, I invite anyone who so desires to get in line and take a turn going under the sword. Many years' experience have taught me how to stop my *bokken* at the last split second should the participant fail to move—yes, this happens—or bow his or her head back under the sword *after* moving the body out of the way. I work with each person until he or she makes a reasonably effective move. Then I bow with respect for his or her courage.

This exercise gives even the beginner a brief opportunity of being in the moment and perhaps a sample of time's malleability. I suspect, however, its unusual appeal is due to more than that. All of us, to one degree or another, know that just to be alive is to be under the sword. We all face death or the possibility of serious injury or loss; we just can't predict when it will come. We know this and we forget. Again and again we forget. And maybe it's somehow necessary for us to take refuge in the security of our forgetfulness. But to deny the sword, to deny the inevitability of death, makes it easier for us to squander the life we are given. To acknowledge that we are under the sword is to realize that we are always in the moment, that this life is an incredible gift, and that it is altogether too short.

A Code for the Modern Samurai

My friend Leo Litwak served as a medic with Patton's forces in Europe and he has told me more than once that the smell of a cup of hot coffee on a snowy morning in Germany long ago is more real, more vivid than almost any present moment. And I, too, have wartime memories that never grow dim—the earth tilting hugely as I turn onto the target, the tracer bullets floating up toward me from the dark green grove, the tracers from my guns floating down past them, sweet, silent sparks of golden orange in the crystal morning light, the plane next to me hit but still flying. And in the distance, the sea, the wonder, the forever of it filling my throat.

What a pity it is that war, with its terrible suffering and devastation, should often be more vivid than peace. In war, your comrades mean everything to you, life is unsure and thus precious, and you know that the sword is raised above you. Now it is peace. Your friends still mean everything, life is still precious, and look—why didn't you notice it?—there's the sword, still raised above you.

Descended from the samurai tradition, aikido offers all of us, not just those who practice the martial arts, the possibility of becoming a new kind of samurai. What might the code of this modern-day samurai be?

- The Modern Samurai is not one who goes to war or kills people, but one who is dedicated to the creation of a more vivid peace.
- The Modern Samurai honors the traditional samurai virtues: loyalty, integrity, dignity, courtesy, courage, prudence, and benevolence.
- The Modern Samurai seeks to prevent violence of every type or, should violence occur, to transform it into harmony.

• The Modern Samurai takes full responsibility for his or her actions.

• The Modern Samurai pursues self-mastery through will, patience, and diligent practice.

• The Modern Samurai respects and values the human individual and the entire web of life on this planet. To serve others is of the highest good. To freely give and accept nourishment from life is the warrior's challenge.

• The Modern Samurai seeks the inner freedom that comes from the study of art, culture, and the wisdom of the ages.

• The Modern Samurai reveres the spiritual realm that lies beyond appetites and appearances.

• The Modern Samurai aims to achieve control and act with abandon.

• The Modern Samurai is willing to take calculated risks to realize his or her potential and further the common good.

• The Modern Samurai realizes that being a warrior doesn't mean winning or even succeeding. It does mean putting your life on the line. It means risking and failing and risking again, as long you live.

• The Modern Samurai cherishes life and thus conducts his or her affairs in such a manner as to be prepared at every moment for death.

Ready to Die; Ready to Live Fully

The last of these is perhaps the most urgent. Ideally, the traditional samurai awakened every morning, all affairs in order, prepared to die that day. For the Modern Samurai, this means something as straightforward as having an up-to-date will, making sure that matters of succession have been handled and other practical requests made clear to your probable survivors. Perhaps more important, do you feel current and complete in all your business, personal, and intimate relationships? Is there anything that needs to be said that you haven't said, anything that needs to be cleared up that you just haven't had time to deal with?

A relationship can be complete if you're sure that you never need to or want to see a formerly close person again. But consider carefully: Do you really feel complete? Or is there something that needs to be said? Have you told your mother, father, sister, brother, or other loved one that you love him or her lately? Would you feel incomplete at the moment of your death not having said those ordinary and absolutely essential words?

There are many forms of communication available today. You can write a letter, send a fax or an E-mail, pick up a phone and punch in a number. You can do it before midnight tonight, not to serve death but to live a more joyful life.

As a Modern Samurai, you know the sword is raised. To step aside when it comes down on you, you'll need to be clear and present, to have no regrets or other considerations. And when the moment eventually arrives that you can no longer step aside—as it must—you can meet your death as a samurai, with no regrets.

CHAPTER 21

The Beginner

This book, as I've said from the beginning, isn't just about aikido. The life lessons that can be drawn from that revolutionary art apply to every human endeavor—and this includes the crucial importance of all beginnings: your first day at school, at college, at a new job; your first flying lesson, music lesson, dance lesson; the day you leave home to make your own way in the world. Knowing less than anyone else, no matter what you're beginning, you're the one who enjoys the incomparable privilege of having the most to learn. The white belt worn by beginning martial artists is a perfect symbol for all beginners. It is the pure white page of the book not yet written, the life ahead of you still to be lived. Take, for example, a first class in aikido.

Embarking on a Journey to Parts Unknown

You stand at the edge of the mat, not knowing quite what to do. Your brand-new white cotton *gi* feels strange to you; the material is stiff and uncomfortable. The senior student who outfitted you said it would shrink, but right now the trousers and sleeves seem much too long. That, and the fact that your *gi* is whiter than anyone else's, makes you feel conspicuous and uneasy. At the same time, there's a thrill of excitement and eager anticipation in the center of your abdomen, the kind of feeling you might get when embarking on a journey to parts unknown.

As you stand there at the edge of the mat, you see the other students doing warm-up exercises and stretches you've never before encountered. Some of them are throwing themselves head over heels then effortlessly coming back up to a standing position. It's hard to imagine yourself ever doing that. You glance down at the gleaming white belt you're wearing. The knot you've tied in the front seems all wrong.

Just then the senior student who outfitted you comes over to help. Yes, the knot *is* wrong. She smiles and shows you how to tie it. She tells you she will stay with you during this first class and help you get started. She tells you it's perfectly natural to feel clumsy in the beginning; everybody does. She tells you that the first thing is just to step on the mat and bow to the large photograph of aikido's founder. She steps on the mat and bows. It's a simple, unpretentious bow. She turns and smiles at you. You step on the mat and bow.

The Beginner's Assets

No matter how clumsy and uneasy he or she might feel, even the rawest beginner comes equipped with those impressive assets common to all of us. The human brain is the most complex, most highly organized entity in the known universe. Though slower and less precise than a computer, it enjoys a creative capacity that is, for all practical purposes, infinite. Seventy percent of your neocortex is uncommitted to any specific task and thus is available for anything you're willing to learn, for thoughts never before thought, for creations in fields as yet unknown. All it takes to operate this extraordinary organ is ten watts of electricity, just about enough to power a tiny night light. Yet with those ten watts you can light up the world.

Your senses are less specialized than those of other animals (the distance vision of the eagle, the canine's uncanny senses of hearing and smell, the sensitive paws of the raccoon), but your total sensorium is the most balanced and highly integrated in the animal kingdom. And through training you can develop uncanny sensory sensitivities; witness the wine taster, the perfume tester, the professional cloth feeler who can identify a piece of cloth by rubbing it with a stick.

You were born with a God-given right to move skillfully, gracefully, and joyfully. We have been taught that we are puny and helpless compared to other animals of the jungle, but this is not true. Imagine a mammal decathlon with the following events; sprinting, endurance running, long jumping, high jumping, hurdling, swimming, deep diving, gymnastics, striking, and throwing. Other animals would win most of the individual events, but a well-trained man or woman would have the best overall score. And the human would quite possibly win three of the individual events: endurance running, gymnastics, and throwing. In a long chase, human runners have caught the horse, kangaroo, deer, zebra, pronghorn antelope (one of the fastest creatures on earth), and many more. Even if you've been robbed of your athletic birthright by our sedentary lifestyle and aversive physical education, you can now begin to reclaim it.

Putting It Up on the Mat

In body, mind, and spirit, each human being exists on the leading edge, as far as we can tell, of some fifteen billion years of inorganic and organic evolution. Each of us is, as O Sensei said, a miniature universe, recapitulating the entire history of the larger universe: the joining of subatomic particles to create atoms, then atoms coming together to make molecules, then further joinings to create complex molecules, simple living cells, more complex cells, then increasingly complex life forms having the powers of sensation, impulse, emotion, and finally the emergence of self-aware consciousness and the explosive blossoming of language, art, technology, and the awareness of God. In this blossoming, we stand not only at the leading edge of the known universe but at the early stages of a meta-evolution now moving us at an ever-accelerating pace toward some unknown destiny.

Do we dare believe this is so? How can we dare not to?

We have become aware not only of what is but of what could be. We know the inevitability of death and are therefore filled with a fierce passion to live, to love, to create, and to feel deeply. We have experienced the sting of tragedy as well as the self-existent delight that exists somewhere deep within each of us, even on the darkest day. We realize—how can we help but realize?—that we are both flawed and magnificent, and that we are mostly unrealized potential.

I believe that the aikido philosophy can be of great help in realizing our potential, especially in this uncertain age. We urgently need more balance and centeredness. We need more positive alternatives to conflict. We need to model strong and beautiful rather than contentious and ugly behaviors for our young people. We need to return the word *power* to its original roots: "to be able." We need to create a more vivid peace. We need to experience our oneness with all beings and with the universe itself. We need to work toward creating a society based on the realization of the potential of its every citizen. We need to own, to take responsibility for our lives.

The simple yet profound teachings that come from aikido can be successfully applied to whatever path we walk in life. But all of our good intentions will be wasted unless we are willing to put ourselves up on the mat, to be beginners.

Earlier in this book I suggested that we see the training mat as the world. Let's turn that around and view the world as our training mat. For your final life lesson, spend some time deciding what you believe, really believe, in the depths of your heart and what you want to do with your life. Then consider the possibility that you can *always* put it on the mat—your body, your beliefs, your life—and that every day, every hour, every second offers a new beginning—but only if you're willing to be a beginner, to wear your white belt. Now step on the mat. Start practicing. And if the practice is congenial to your truest and deepest impulses, keep practicing for as long as you live.

APPENDIX

An Experiment in Human Transformation

On January 4, 1992, Michael Murphy and I convened a two-year experimental class in what we called Integral Transformative Practice (ITP). There were thirty-three people in the first year's class and thirty in the second, with thirteen staying for both years, making up a total of fifty participants. The class was *integral* in that it integrated body, mind, heart, and soul, and also integrated the practice with each participant's home and job; *transformative* in that it aimed at positive change ranging from the ordinary to the extraordinary; and a *practice* in that it constituted a nontrivial activity continued on a regular, long-term basis.

We were prompted to conduct this experiment, in part, by many years' acquaintance with intense group experiences that lasted only a weekend or a week and seemed to have strongly transformative effects. The effects were real enough; the only problem was that after a few days they began fading away and soon were gone. Our experience and research had strongly suggested that long-term change demanded diligent, patient, long-term practice. Our respect for the transformative power of such practice was reflected in my 1991 book, *Mastery*, which sang the praises of practice primarily for its own sake, and in Murphy's encyclopedic work, *The Future of the Body*, published in 1992. Murphy's 800-page book grew out of a fifteen-year study of extraordinary human functioning. It was drawn from nearly ten thousand documents and contains some 2500 citations, plus a bibliography eighty-six pages in length. The book ends with a list of guiding principles for integral practices. One of these principles states that integral practices generally require several mentors rather than a single guru. To this end, we brought in Erik Van Riswold and Annie Styron Leonard, both experienced aikidoists and group leaders, to join us as teachers.

The class met at the Aikido of Tamalpais dojo every Saturday morning for two hours and also held two overnight retreats. The Saturday classes included group support, discussion of assigned readings, LET exercises similar to those in this book, and a 40-minute ITP Kata, which I created for the practice. The Japanese word *kata* means simply "form" and stands for any series of exercises performed continuously in a certain sequence. This kata involves exercises for the body, mind, and spirit. You can trace its lineage to hatha yoga, aikido, modern exercise physiology, Progressive Relaxation, visualization research, and meditation research. It offers the following benefits:

- balances and centers the body and psyche
- provides a full body warm-up
- articulates all the joints
- offers a comprehensive course of stretches
- includes three essential strength exercises
- presents numerous opportunities for deep, rhythmic breathing
- provides a session of deep relaxation
- includes a period of transformative imaging for creating positive changes in body and psyche
- conclude with meditation

Members of the ITP class were asked to make four affirmations of positive change. The fourth affirmation for everyone was "My entire being is balanced, vital, and healthy." The affirmations were not casually tossed off but thoughtfully considered over a period of weeks before being signed. Careful records were kept concerning the participant's condition in regard to each affirmation at the time the affirmations were signed and again at the end of the year.

All participants committed themselves to attend meetings regularly and also to deepen their practice on the days between meetings. They agreed to

maintain their individual autonomy and authority while committing themselves to the group in vision and practice;

do the ITP Kata at least five times a week;

do at least three hours of aerobic exercise every week in increments of at least thirty minutes. In addition, they agreed to do whatever flexibility, strength, balance, coordination, concentration, and relaxation exercise would be necessary to realize their affirmations;

be conscious of everything they ate and consider the many benefits of a diet low in fat and high in fiber;

read all written material assigned by the teachers and, commensurate with their own best judgment, seek to integrate it into their practice;

stay current in their relationships with teachers and fellow participants and take care of emotional needs in appropriate and healthy ways; and

include their affirmations in their kata and seek in all appropriate and healthy ways to manifest those affirmations in body and being.

Significant Results

We kept careful records of all changes and at the end of each year engaged the services of a statistician to analyze the figures. We were struck by the strong correlation between adherence to the program and success in realizing affirmations and by the significant improvement in overall health. There were also some unexpected findings that suggested the importance of what we call "mind" or "intentionality" in positive human change. For example, how focused participants were while doing the ITP Kata seemed to be more important than the number of times they did the kata and how conscious they were of what they ate more important than exactly what they ate, though both were important.

In addition, there were positive changes that challenged conventional explanation. A forty-five-year-old woman with a long family history of cataracts reversed her own cataracts over the two years of the program. A fifty-seven-year-old woman who suffered from functional epilepsy was averaging one *grand mal* seizure a month when the program started. She has had none since. A forty-six-year-old man increased his leg strength by 140 percent without changing his physical exercise regimen. The positive changes were by no means entirely physical. For example, one woman manager significantly increased the amount of time she could spend in the "flow state" while on the job.

Starting Your Own ITP Group

At the end of the second year, we four teachers stepped back and handed over the practice to the students. Murphy and I spent the next two years completing a book, *The Life We Are Given*. During the same period, I produced a video-tape, *The Tao of Practice*, on which I teach the ITP Kata.

Publication of the book and tape has made it possible for people to start their own ITP practice groups or to practice alone. We have received more than fifteen hundred letters inquiring about ITP, many of which tell of practice groups the letter writers have started in the United States and over-seas. We have no way of knowing just how many groups are now active, but we estimate there are at least forty. To make it possible for people to find others in their area who might want to start a group, as well as to provide other information about ITP, Murphy and I have opened a Website (see below).

A doctoral candidate is currently carrying on a sophisticated research project on the ITP group descended from our original group, and the Stanford Center for Research in Disease Prevention of the Stanford University School of Medicine has written a proposal for a large-scale study on the use of ITP as an intervention to elicit and sustain optimal health for individuals age fifty-five to seventy-nine. We have reason to believe that Integral Transformative Practice can help people of all ages and backgrounds to realize more of their potential for good health in the broadest sense of the word.

To get information on ITP or on how to order The Tao of Practice, visit our Website at itp-life.com, or write ITP, P.O. Box 609, Mill Valley, CA 94942

SELECTED READINGS

Paul Davies. *The Mind of God: The Scientific Basis for a Rational World*. Simon & Schuster, 1992.

Taisen Deshimaru. *The Zen Way to the Martial Arts*. E. P Dutton, 1982.

Peter Farb. *Humankind*. Houghton Mifflin Co., 1978.

James Gleick, *Chaos: Making a New Science*. Viking, 1987

George Greenstein. *The Symbiotic Universe*. William Morrow & Co. Inc., 1988.

Eugen Herrigel. *Zen in the Art of Archery*. Vintage Books, 1971.

Johan Huizinga. *Homo Ludens: A Study of the Play Element in Culture*. Beacon Press, 1955.

Michio Kaku. *Hyperspace: A Scientific Odyssey Through Parallel Universes, Time Warps, and the 10th Dimension*. Oxford University Press, 1994.

George Leonard. *The Silent Pulse*. Dutton, 1978.

———. *Education and Ecstasy*. North Atlantic Books, 1987

————. *The Ultimate Athlete*. North Atlantic Books, 1990.

————. *Mastery*. Dutton NAL, 1991.

George Leonard and Michael Murphy. *The Life We Are Given*. Tarcher-Putnam, 1995.

Roger Lewin. *In the Age of Mankind*. Smithsonian Institution Press, 1988.

Michael Murphy. *The Future of the Body. Explorations into the Further Reaches of Human Nature*. J. P. Tarcher, Inc. 1992.

Michael Murphy and Steven Donovan. *The Physical and Psychological Effects of Meditation*. Institute of Noetic Sciences, Sausalito, California, 1997

Inozo Nitobe. *Bushido: The Soul of Japan*. Charles E. Tuttle Co., 1969.

Christopher Peterson and Lisa M. Bossio. *Health and Optimism. New Research on the Relationship Between Positive Thinking and Physical Well-Being*. The Free Press, 1991

Mitsugi Saotome, *Aikido and the Harmony of Nature*. Shambhala, 1993.

Martin E. P. Seligman. *Learned Optimism*. Alfred A. Knopf, 1991

Joseph Silk. *The Big Bang* (revised edition). W. H. Freeman, and Co., 1994.

John Stevens. *Abundant Peace: The Biography of Morihei Ueshiba*. Shambhala, 1987

————. *The Sword of No Sword: Life of the Master Warrior Tesshu*. Shambhala, 1984.

Kisshomaru Ueshiba. *Aikido*. Hozansha Publishing Co., Ltd, 1969.

————. *The Spirit of Aikido*. Kodansha International, 1984.

Karlfried Graf Von Durckheim. *Hara: The Vital Center in Man*. Mandala Books: Unwin Paperbacks, 1980.

Ken Wilber. *Sex, Ecology, Spirituality: The Spirit of Evolution*. Shambhala, 1995.

ACKNOWLEDGMENTS

My wife, Annie Styron Leonard, who holds a black belt in aikido and is an LET trainer, gave me unusually perceptive readings and unfailing support during the entire process of writing this book.

I'm especially indebted to my teacher, Mitsugi Saotome, an *uchi-deshi* (live-in student) of aikido's founder for fifteen years and one of the world's premier martial artists. Saotome Sensei's book, *Aikido and the Harmony of Nature*, a profound and wide-ranging exploration of the philosophy underlying this revolutionary martial art, has served as a major source in the writing of this book. I also thank the teacher who continues his lineage, Hiroshi Ikeda. I'm always astonished by the subtlety and sheer magic of his aikido and warmed by his humor and compassion.

My first teacher, Robert Nadeau, introduced me not only to aikido as a martial art, but also to the notion of presenting its lessons to non–martial artists. His ingenious translations of aikido clearly show its application to daily life. The elegance and precision of Frank Doran's techniques have inspired me and many other aikidoists.

My Aikido of Tamalpais partner, Wendy Palmer, and I have shared twenty-seven years of aikido friendship and harmony along with many musical and martial arts adventures, some of which appear in the previous pages. Richard Heckler, a close companion on the path, has delighted me with his graceful aikido and prose. Thanks as always to my close friends and constant advisors: Michael Murphy, Leo Litwak, and John and Julia Poppy.

I have learned more from the many students who have trained at Aikido of Tamalpais than they have learned from me and I would like to list them all by name. But that list would be far too long and I wouldn't take the chance of leaving even one of them out. *Domo arigato!*

Finally, let me thank my agent, Frederick Hill, for his impeccable taste and my editor, Brian Tart, for his wise, sensitive, and enthusiastic editing.

 **PLUME**

ALSO BY GEORGE LEONARD

MASTERY Drawing on Zen philosophy and the martial art of Aikido, Leonard explains the process of "Mastery" and how it enables you to reach a higher level of excellence and a deeper sense of satisfaction in anything from sports to your career.

0-452-26756-0